COMMUNICATION
AND CULTURAL DOMINATION

COMMUNICATION
AND CULTURAL DOMINATION

HERBERT I. SCHILLER

 INTERNATIONAL ARTS AND SCIENCES PRESS, INC , WHITE PLAINS, N.Y.

To PCH and BZ

An earlier version of Chapter 2 was published in Le Monde
Diplomatique, Paris, September 1975, and also in Instant Research on Peace and Violence, 1975, No. 2, Tampere, Finland.

A section of Chapter 4 was published in Gazette (Amsterdam),
1975, Vol. 21, No. 2.

Library of Congress Catalog Card Number: 76-2916
International Standard Book Number: 0-87332-079-4

Printed in the United States of America

CONTENTS

1955732

ACKNOWLEDGMENTS

At one time or another in its preparation, different parts of the manuscript were read by Eqbal Ahmad, Esther Cohen, Tran Van Dinh, George Gerbner, Cees Hamelink, Mark Lushington, Karl Ola Nilsson, Kaarle Nordenstreng, Dallas Smythe, and Tapio Varis. Their comments helped to clarify many points.

As in the past, I leaned heavily on the constructive criticism, which generally transcended familial loyalty, of Anita, Dan, and Zach Schiller.

The interest and enthusiasm for the themes in this book shown by my students and associates in the Mass Communications Seminar at the Institute for the Science of the Press at the University of Amsterdam in 1973-74 and spring 1975 made me feel that the work was worth pursuing. In addition, the Institute itself provided a supportive atmosphere for writing and research.

My gratitude is due also to friends and colleagues in the International Association for Mass Communication Research who, without necessarily sharing my views, have in recent years offered me a friendly forum. The internationalism thus provided has been, for me, enormously self-sustaining.

Finally, Arnold Tovell's recommendations encouraged me to give the work a coherent form. Brenda Collins generously typed drafts of some of the chapters.

H. I. S.

ACKNOWLEDGMENTS

FOREWORD

The attainment of political independence by more than ninety countries since the Second World War has directed attention to the conditions of economic helplessness and dependency that continue to frustrate the development of at least two-thirds of the world's nations. Two and sometimes three decades of disappointing efforts to extricate themselves from dependency have begun to provoke serious reappraisals in many lands about the entire concept of development.

Though the economic measures of domination — control of capital and markets and of the infrastructure of international finance — are increasingly well understood, the cultural-communications sources of power are just beginning to be faintly perceived. The forces that influence consciousness are decisive determinants of a community's outlook and the nature and direction of its goals. Thus, communications and the flow of messages and imagery within and among nations — especially between developed and dominated states — assume a very special significance. What does it matter if a national movement has struggled for years to achieve liberation if that condition, once gained, is undercut by values and aspirations derived from the apparently vanquished dominator?

For this reason, attention in many nations is beginning to focus on the sources, character, and content of the communication stream that passes between nations and on the flow that is

1

generated inside national states. It is hardly surprising that
most of these flows still reflect and bear the mark (in some
places more clearly than in others) of old imperial connections.
In any case, they almost always reveal aspects of command-
and-obey relationships.

But if the dominated are slowly awakening to the importance
of the cultural-communications component in their struggle for
meaningful existence and independence, the dominators are no
less alert to its significance. Indeed, their awareness may be
outpacing that of their victims. There are compelling reasons
for this.

Profound changes have occurred in the command of global
power in the last ten years. The American empire has suffered
heavy setbacks. Its inability to overcome the National Liberation Front and the People's Democratic Republic of Vietnam
was perhaps its greatest defeat and the source of many of its
current and future troubles.

The disastrous effects of the war in Vietnam on American
capitalism have been far-reaching. At home, the entire political process has become suspect. Inflation and resource mis-
allocations, attributable in part to the concealed (from the people) costs of the war, continue to destabilize the economy and
to create further dangerous economic inequalities in the society. Internationally, rival centers of capitalist strength, though
themselves in crisis, have benefited from the strains on the
United States economy. American hegemony is increasingly
disputed; and, especially in the formerly colonial (Third World)
countries, opposition to continued economic domination intensifies.

Facing these already considerable but still developing crises,
American managers of empire have been pressed to improvise
and accommodate. To be sure, they have resisted fiercely any
encroachments on the core of their power — the euphemistically
labeled multinational corporations, whose worldwide plant and
facilities now exceed $160 billion in market value.

Yet, limited in the application of military force by counter-
vailing power and confronting multiplying challenges in many

hitherto hospitable areas, American imperialism has been developing complementary, if not alternate, strategies and instrumentation for safeguarding its unstable and increasingly menaced global positions. The ideological sphere receives ever more attention.

Assisted by the sophisticated communications technology developed in the militarily oriented space program, techniques of persuasion, manipulation, and cultural penetration are becoming steadily more important, and more deliberate, in the exercise of American power. In addition, the accumulation of fifty years of domestic marketing expertise is now let loose on the world at large.

The marketing system developed to sell industry's outpouring of (largely inauthentic) consumer goods is now applied as well to selling globally ideas, tastes, preferences, and beliefs. In fact, in advanced capitalism's present stage, the production and dissemination of what it likes to term "information" become major and indispensable activities, by any measure, in the overall system. Made-in-America messages, imagery, life-styles, and information techniques are being internationally circulated and, equally important, globally imitated.

Today, multinational corporations are the global organizers of the world economy; and information and communications are vital components in the system of administration and control. Communication, it needs to be said, includes much more than messages and the recognizable circuits through which the messages flow. It defines social reality and thus influences the organization of work, the character of technology, the curriculum of the educational system, formal and informal, and the use of "free" time — actually, the basic social arrangements of living. It is a measure of the effectiveness of the control processes that recognition of their existence is only now beginning to be appreciated and understood beyond a tiny, informed circle.

Accordingly, the time ahead will surely be a period of growing cultural-communications struggle — intra- and internationally — between those seeking the end of domination and those striving to maintain it. The intention of this work is to

assist, in a very modest way, in the outcome of this struggle.
It does this, I hope, by describing the process of cultural domination, some of the elements that constitute it, and the mechanisms of its operation and extension, and finally, offering some
general observations on possible means of resisting it. The
analysis begins with a brief description of the basic relationships that structure power domestically and internationally and,
consequently, cultural contacts among peoples and nations.

CULTURAL DOMINATION: SOURCES, CONTEXT AND CURRENT STYLES

"...we are on the threshold of a <u>new kind</u> <u>of cultural diplomacy</u>."

— Report of Panel on International Information, Education, and Cultural Relations

In his comprehensive and illuminating study of the "modern world system," Immanuel Wallerstein (<u>1</u>) finds three basic elements. For him, the system consists of
— "(metaphorically)...a single market within which calculations of maximum profitability are made and which therefore determine over some long run the amount of productive activity, the degree of specialization, the modes of payment for labor, goods and services, and utility of technological invention";
— "...a series of state structures, of varying degrees of strength (both within their boundaries and vis-à-vis other entities in the world-system)..."
— "...appropriation of surplus labor [that] takes place in such a way that there are not two, but three tiers to the exploitative process."
Cultural imperialism today can begin to be understood, I believe, by reference to these key elements. It develops in a <u>world</u> system within which there is a single market, and the terms and character of production are determined in the core of that market and radiate outward. National states exist and impinge on the "pure" workings of the world system. Ordinarily their interventions benefit (or seek to benefit) the interests of the dominant classes in their own domains. And for the preservation of the system, internationally and within each constituent state in the system, the maintenance of an intermediary layer or layers is essential. Third forces, middle classes, and

informational pluralism are the catchwords and necessities of
system maintenance.

The cultural-communications sector of the world system necessarily develops in accordance with and facilitates the aims
and objectives of the general system. A largely one-directional
flow of information from core to periphery represents the reality of power. So, too, does the promotion of a single language —
English. A rapid, all-encompassing communication technology
(satellites and computers) is sought, discovered, and developed.
Its utilization exhibits a close correspondence to the structure
and the needs of the dominant elements in the core of the system.

We shall return to these matters. At this point it is enough
to note that these instruments, which presently serve and enhance the system of domination, could, at a later time, provide
a basis for the transformation that would replace the prevailing
exploitative structure.

There is yet another complicating factor that especially affects the cultural-communications sphere of the world system.
Cultural-informational outputs are largely, though not entirely,
determined by the same market imperatives that govern the
overall system's production of goods and services. Yet, as we
are well aware, cultural-informational outputs represent much
more than conventional units of personal-consumption goods:
they are also embodiments of the ideological features of the
world capitalist economy. They serve, extremely effectively,
to promote and develop popular support for the values, or at
least the artifacts, of the system. For example, David Ogilvy (2),
founder of the powerful Ogilvy and Mather advertising agency,
in a lavish endorsement of the Reader's Digest, commented:
"The magazine exports the best in American life.... In my
opinion, the Digest is doing as much as the United States Information Agency to win the battle for men's minds."

What, then, have been the dynamics of the cultural-informational
processes within the context of the modern world capitalist
economy, particularly since the end of the Second World War?

Elsewhere I have examined the objectives and operations of

multinational corporations (MNCs) in communications. (3) Here
it may suffice to repeat that the basic economic organizational
unit in the modern world capitalist economy is the MNC. A few
hundred of these giant agglomerations of capital, largely American owned, dominate the global market in the production and
distribution of goods and services. Most significantly from our
standpoint, this dominance extends to the production and dissemination of communications-cultural outputs as well.

These aggressive business empires organize the world market as best they can, subject, of course, to the uneven and partial constraints of national regulation, often minimal, and differ-
ential levels of economic development in the areas in which they
are active. In furthering their goals of securing worldwide markets and unimpeded profitability, they are compelled to influence, and if possible dominate, every cultural and informational
space that separates them from total control of their global/
national environment. This is not a short-run necessity: it is a
permanent condition that arises out of a market system and the
way that system establishes its priorities and consequently its
rewards and sanctions.

Read (4), analyzing the activities of what he terms "America's mass media mercantilists" (why not imperialists?), insists that economics, and economics alone, accounts for the
worldwide dissemination and penetration of U.S.-made cultural-
communications outputs:

> Every commercial organization, whether it manufac-
> tures cars or produces films, has a so-called bottom
> line, that is, the last line on its financial ledger showing
> either profit or loss.... It is the "bottom" line that mo-
> tivates American mass media organizations to seek ac-
> cess to foreign markets and it is the predominant per-
> spective from which they analyze the conditions of en-
> try.... [And, again] access sought is profits sought.

Having demonstrated this beyond a doubt, Read believes that
he has refuted the existence of <u>cultural</u> imperialism because,

indisputably, the process of penetration has an economic basis. But such purely economic determinism overlooks many consequences of the process it seeks to analyze. Though the economic imperative initiates the cultural envelopment, the impact extends far beyond the profit-seeking objectives of some huge media monopolies and cultural conglomerates, important and powerful as these combines are. The cultural penetration that has occurred in recent decades embraces all the socializing institutions of the affected host area. And though this, too, occurs mostly for economic reasons, the impact inevitably is felt throughout the realm of individual and social consciousness in the penetrated provinces.

Consider, for example, the business practices of the (statistically) typical multinational corporation. The enterprise operates facilities in a couple of dozen countries. Decisions, whether highly centralized in the home country (ordinarily the United States) or left to relatively autonomous plant managers and executives in the various branches scattered over three or four continents, must be coordinated. More importantly, they must follow assumptions and common understandings agreed on by the top-level management, wherever it is situated. How is this uniformity of perspective assured? Largely, as one writer puts it, through the "transmission of business culture."

Several elements are at work in this process. There are: the implantation of expatriate executive staff; business education within both the firm and the schools in the host country that are established to provide indigenous managers and workers for international companies; the adoption of English as the lingua franca of international business (for example, Philips, the giant Dutch electrical equipment multinational corporation, now uses English as the language for all internal correspondence [5]); and the utilization of the talents and energies of (mostly) U.S.-owned international advertising agencies and market research and polling firms.

The result of these diverse but interconnected activities and relationships is a cultural take-over of the penetrated society. The impulse that produces cultural domination originates with commercial imperatives, but this in no way diminishes the impact on the cultural landscape of the penetrated society. In fact, even if the latter begins to develop its own variety of cultural outputs, the initiating force of corporate capitalism's drive for profitability cannot be escaped.

Once the take-over process has begun, it is extended to all the institutional networks of the receiving society. The infrastructure of socialization is closely interknit, and a current in one channel quickly flows into or seeks support in another. Besides, the modern world system is unrelenting in its demands and necessities. From the time a region/nation is absorbed fully into the system, it is compelled — given some latitude in the national circumstances of developmental level and degree of political independence — to adapt its production, its working force, its rewards, its concept of efficiency, its degree of specialization, its investments, and its resource priorities to the world capitalist economy.

To be sure, an international structure of domination, i.e., colonialism, existed for hundreds of years. What is being considered here is the transformation of that system — in its realignments of power centers, its changed sources of exploitation, and its modern mode of organization and control.

In this sense, the concept of cultural imperialism today best describes the sum of the processes by which a society is brought into the modern world system and how its dominating stratum is attracted, pressured, forced, and sometimes bribed into shaping social institutions to correspond to, or even promote, the values and structures of the dominating center of the system.

The public media* are the foremost example of operating

---

*Public media is the term used here to describe what are generally referred to as the mass media. I find myself in agreement with Cees Hamelink that public media better explain, or at least permit the possibility of understanding, the processes by which messages are made public. (Cees Hamelink, Perspectives for Public Communication, Ten Have, Baarn, The Netherlands, 1975. See especially footnote 1, p. 92.)

enterprises that are used in the penetrative process. For penetration on a significant scale the media themselves must be
captured by the dominating/penetrating power. This occurs
largely through the commercialization of broadcasting. (The
press invariably is commercial at the outset.)

Latin America, for example, represents a peripheral region
in which (with the exception of Cuba) broadcasting is thoroughly
commercialized and serves fully the requirements of the multinational corporations and their indigenous counterparts and
supporters. Two researchers report, for example, that Vene-
zuelan commercial television content "is, for the most part,
advertising, violence and imported films." (6)

Western Europe, itself part of the core of the world capitalist
economy, has also moved toward the commercialization of its
broadcast media, reflecting the insatiable market needs of its
own business system, to say nothing of its substantial American
component. Once commercial, a series of economic pressures
thereafter ensure that the broadcast media everywhere will
carry the cultural material produced in the core areas (the
United States, Great Britain, the Federal Republic of Germany,
and a few other centers). Imitations of that material may appear when and if the indigenous broadcast/film/print industries
demand a share in their home market. Directly or indirectly,
the outcome is the same. The content and style of the programming, however adapted to local conditions, bear the ideological
imprint of the main centers of the capitalist world economy.

Disney products are prototypic:

> Disney, like the missionary Peace Corpsman or "good-
> will ambassador" of his Public Relations men, has learned
> the native lingoes — he is fluent in eighteen of them at the
> moment. In Latin America he speaks Spanish and Portu-
> guese; and he speaks it from magazines which are slightly
> different, in other ways, from those produced elsewhere
> and at home. There are, indeed, at least four different
> Spanish language editions of the Disney comic. The differ-
> ences between them do not affect the basic content.... (7)

Similarly, the character and organization of education and scientific research in core and peripheral countries alike are compelled to adapt to and serve the requirements of the multinational corporate economy. Education in the advanced, capitalist states is arranged to produce managers, administrators, and skilled workers for the multinational corporations and the state bureaucracy. Similar, if less efficient, educational structures are established outside the core region.

One of the priority tasks of the Agency for International Development has been to organize schools and institutes, patterned after the North American model, in Third World countries. Sometimes, major American universities, in what appears as educational philanthropy, assist in establishing centers outside the United States. Journalism schools, for example, have proliferated throughout Latin America, many of them helped into existence and subsidized on a continuing basis by funds from the United States (8), flowing through sometimes obscure channels.

At the highest level of training — for corporate managers and executives — the most prestigious business schools in U.S. universities have taken an active part in internationalizing their instruction. The Harvard Business School has an affiliate management school in Lausanne, Switzerland; and another management school in Lausanne also has intellectual links to Harvard. New York University has organized a cooperative venture with the London Business School, affiliated with the University of London, and with the Ecole Des Hautes Etudes Commerciales at Jouy-en-Josas, near Paris. "Graduates of the Program in the first two years," it is reported, "have found jobs easily. They have been hired by such concerns as First National City Bank, Morgan Guaranty Trust, Irving Trust, First Philadelphia Bank, Booz, Allen and Hamilton, ICI, and the French Industrial Development Agency." (9)

In other institutes in Europe, the "staff and alumni from Harvard and Wharton are an influential if not dominant group within the faculty, and, in most cases, teaching and reading reflect a decidedly American business ethos." All of this leads inescapably

to the conclusion that "The coming generation of top managers
in Europe, all more or less similarly trained to put the commercial interests of their enterprises above other considerations, are increasingly divorced from their particular national
framework, and reflect, if anything, the business philosophy of
the ruling United States schools." (10)

By no means is this influence restricted to Europe. For example, the Financial Times (October 3, 1973) describes the Department of Business Administration of the American University
in Beirut as "the Middle East's Harvard... [It] provides the local intellectual cream for the area."

More than the education of future business leaders and government administrators in the capitalist world economy is being shaped by the MNCs' needs. The organization of work in
general and the perspectives and outlooks related thereto are
also focal points for supervision and intrusion. One researcher,
Rita Cruise O'Brien (11), has been examining the transfer of institutional forms and organizational structures from the metropolitan (core) countries to the less-developed societies (periphery) in the crucial field of broadcasting. She observes, "Organizations like the BBC and RTF, NBC and CBS exported not only
their structures but their philosophies of operation, the traces
of which remain in varying degrees in Africa, Asia and Latin
America. These traces are reinforced through continued transfers of personnel, training forms and imported programmes or
programme types."

Along with these arrangements come the highly developed
techniques and perspectives of professionalization. Professionalization as it is known and practiced in the United States and
Western Europe is one of the strongest means of segmenting
the working force. It introduces differentiation and competitive-
ness and promotes a (false) notion of objective and apolitical job
activity and decision-making. As O'Brien (11) notes, "The process of professionalization in broadcasting [as elsewhere] may
itself have introduced a new constraint resistant to changes in
the organizational structure.... There seems no better way of
protecting broadcast training as it is than arguing against

changes which would 'lower the professional standards.'"

Despecialization, open admission to recruitment, and work initiatives from the bottom up would clearly be in opposition to the general structural and ideational requirements of the modern, capitalist, world economy.

When countries seek the advice (for which they pay a pretty sum) of American business consulting firms, what they receive in concentrated form is the message their students absorb in their studies in the schools and institutes organized by, or under the influence of, the same corporate auspices.

A similar condition affects the entire scientific enterprise in peripheral and semiperipheral areas of the modern capitalist world economy. Here, too, an "international scientific market," as Juan Corradi (12) describes it, operates. This market, if less structured and less accessible to ordinary inquiry, conforms to rules no different from those that characterize more conventional markets. Thus, the areas of scientific interest are determined by the needs and the resource decisions made in the power centers (corporate, state bureaucratic, and military) of the core capitalist nations. Accordingly, certain areas are regarded as worthy of attention and receive generous financial support. Other lines of research, no matter how potentially exciting scientifically, are left to languish or remain undeveloped if the power nuclei consider them unpromising.

It is understood that the needs of the people in the periphery are always in this latter category. More harmful still, scientific workers in the dependent regions are, consciously or not (it makes no difference), tied into the network of research interests and priorities established by the international scientific market. Scientists in these areas inevitably either leave, if they are regarded as topflight, to join the higher-paying and allegedly more stimulating research environment in the core area or else stay behind to work on similar projects, but generally in a lesser role and often as mere "gatherers of data" for processing elsewhere. (12) Whichever the case, the needs of the dependent regions remain unmet; and the perspectives of their scientific communities are shaped by their external dominators.

Equally significant, the technology that ensues from much of this research also is unrepresentative of, sometimes incompatible with, the urgent needs of most of the people in the perimeter. More will be said about this later.

In the modern world economy, the developmental process is viewed and applied as the means by which the class structure of the core is replicated in the periphery. One of the most effective ways in which this is achieved is through tourism, which in itself represents a powerful communication channel. The spokesmen of dominant international economic and financial institutions are unanimous in advising and encouraging decision-makers in peripheral nations to develop and broaden their countries' tourist industries as one sure way of obtaining otherwise scarce (withheld) resources.

Tourism as managed in the capitalist world economy serves several ends, all beneficial to the dominant order. It provides relatively cheap diversion to the middle and lower middle classes of the industrialized core nations. Indeed, the geographic mobility that tourism offers serves as a principal attraction of the overall system, which argues successfully that geographic mobility is the definition of freedom and liberty. At the same time, tourism is a source of profit to the monopolistic enterprises that service the traffic, most of these enterprises being based in the core countries. In addition, it enlists and further develops a small and active, though parasitic, entrepreneurial segment in the targeted country.

Perez (13) has described local class interests that interact with the external dominators in the Caribbean area:

> [Tourism] rests on the active collaboration of West Indian elites with metropolitan agencies. National leaders have not only been incapable of reversing the tourist tide but, in many cases, have been its principal promoters and beneficiaries. Landowning groups have benefited enormously from rising land values. Commercial and financial sectors linked to the import aspects of tourism par-

ticipate profitably in the travel industry. These groups collectively form the national elites whose own access to internal hegemony has been a function of their dependence. With the support of metropolitan agencies, West Indian leaders, in the epoch of decolonization and national liberation struggles, have led their societies into the sixteenth century. (P. 142)

An outcome of most tourism is to transform the local setting and its activities, whatever they may be, into some salable goods or atmosphere. In "pure" tourism, everything — people, customs, ceremonies, food, clothing, art, household ornamentation — is for sale. The community itself becomes one huge market. Moreover, the transformation of the economy to a total dependency condition parallels, in some countries, the distortions of an earlier age around a different "industry." We quote Perez (13) again, with reference to the West Indies:

Monoculture, white-black superordinate-subordinate relations, and the organization of society around the gratification of metropolitan needs — all essential characteristics of plantation culture — find immediate counterparts in the tourist culture. The relief of slave quarters against the Great House finds a contemporary parallel in the hovels of downtown Kingston [Jamaica] against the luxury hotel skyline. Real estate speculation and soaring land values have driven the coastal population into the mountainous interiors in a manner reminiscent of the flight of plantation slaves a little more than a century ago. (P. 138)

An additional factor today is the collapse of the time dimension. Developments that may once have taken decades to mature now occur overnight. This can be observed in the fusing of major, commercialized sports, tourism, and modern communications. Joint packages are concocted in which the sports activity is the chief lure. The locale of the event becomes an esoteric background factor, put on display by its own local elite as a

suitable place for tourist bargains in the future. Recent "international" boxing matches are illustrative of this phenomenon.

Zaire, for example, is chosen as the site for a championship
fight before a worldwide TV audience. The promoters of these
extravagantly profitable enterprises jump from one dependent
state to another. Time details one of these forays: "King [the
promoter] has made his deals with governments. Shrewd enough
to realize that championship bouts featuring Ali are the kind of
promotion that developing nations like to stage, King has courted
heads of state in Cairo, Tehran, Lusaka (Zambia), Manila and
Kuala Lumpur." (14)

The arrangements in Kuala Lumpur are equally instructive:
Harun, the Malaysian promoter, says, "we put up $2.5 million
for Ali [the champion], half a million for Bugner [the challenger]
in order to project Malaysia to the world." Who oversees this
projection? "Harun, formerly an attorney, operates Tinju Duvia
Sdn., which translates into World Boxing Ltd., and also is the
chief minister of the State of Selangor, one of the 14 states in
the Federation of Malaysia.... [He] formed a group of Malaysian bankers to finance the fight." (15)

In such accounts we have the explicit mechanics of contemporary cultural imperialism. The world system is the theater,
and the action moves from the center to the edge. It is undertaken with the mutual consent, even solicitation, of the indigenous rulers, either in the core, the semiperiphery, or the periphery. These rulers strive eagerly to push their people and
their nations into the world capitalist economy.

It is for this reason that it may be inappropriate to describe
the contemporary mechanics of cultural control as the outcome
of "invasion," though I, too, have used this term in the past.
Dagnino (16) writes:

> ...the effects of cultural dependence on the lives of Latin
> Americans are not a consequence of an "invasion" led by
> a foreign "enemy," but of a choice made by their own rul-
> ing class, in the name of national development. Through
> this choice, national life and national culture are sub-

ordinated to the dynamics of the international capitalist
system, submitting national cultures to a form of homog-
enization that is considered a requirement for the maintenance of an international system.

What is happening is that "the cultural and ideological homoge-
nization of the world is being pursued not by a single nation but
by an integrated system of different national sectors, committed
to a specific form of socio-economic organization." (16)

It is essential to be aware of the strong, collaborative role of
the ruling groups in the dominated areas of the world capitalist
economy, in what otherwise appears to be a one-way process of
cultural penetration. Still, the active, initiating drives from the
center of the system, from the United States, in particular, cannot be regarded as secondary elements in the process. It is,
after all, the global market imperatives of the U.S.- and West
European-controlled multinational corporations that energize
and organize the world system. It is the imagery and cultural perspectives of this ruling sector in the center that
shape and structure consciousness throughout the system at
large.

This may help to explain the mixture of fury and bewilder-
ment displayed by those responsible for the informational apparatus in the core area when there is any indication of rejection, in outlying regions, of the basic assumptions and arrangements of the central system. How else can we understand the
frenetic attacks on the revolutionary Cambodian leaders when
it appeared to Western officials that that terribly damaged society — pulverized by American bombs and a massive intervention — was withdrawing from the capitalist world system? The
headline across six columns in the International Herald Tribune
on May 9, 1975, read: "Khmer Rouge Evacuates the Cities in
Cambodian Peasant Revolution. Population Sent to Interior:
Urban Economy Abandoned." These events were presented and
analyzed as matters beyond comprehension. Henry Kissinger
termed the first measures of that country's liberation leadership "genocidal."

More than in any previous period, the processes of informational control are, at least in some measure, deliberately organized and applied. Earlier, the market economy, nationally and internationally, was adequate to arrange economic, political, and cultural affairs from the standpoint of those who had the capital, and therefore all the influence. Equally important, the market system had the virtue of appearing apolitical, uncontrolled, and not subject to individual manipulation.

To this day one is assured, at the core and in the periphery, that the market mechanism remains intact, that the basic soundness of the model is unimpaired. However, a note of doubt is beginning to creep into the thinking of the core's leadership. The breakdowns are too frequent and too widespread. The pressure on the world system is intensifying. The national liberation movements, the anti-imperialist wars that end disastrously for the dominators, the deepening economic and resource crises in the center of the system — all these make it impossible to believe in, and to rely exclusively on, "natural" processes of stabilization in the world system.

Reflecting on these concerns, the senior vice president and economist of the Manufacturers Hanover Trust, one of the handful of dominant New York commercial banks, inquires:

> To return to fundamentals, the question that the conservative economists are increasingly asking themselves is whether or not the market enterprise system that has worked so well for us for 200 years is, in fact, a viable system. As we look realistically at the history of the world during this 200 year period we see it spotted with episodes of severe depression — the 1930s was by no means our first serious depression — with periods of growth interspersed between these depressions. Under the political autocracy that has characterized world governments through most of the time until the Second World War, the bargaining position of the workers who are most sadly affected by these depressions has been so weak that there have not been, as a general rule, serious political

disorders accompanying the depressions.

We must now ask ourselves if the twenty-five to thirty years since the Second World War might not be an unusual period. We have prided ourselves during this episode upon having solved the problems of instability that have plagued capitalist economies throughout their history. But in fact have we not just been living during a period of un- usual stability supported on the one hand by a strong U.S. economy and on the other hand by cheap natural resources from the developing countries? If the worst should hap- pen, if the present recovery is only a temporary interlude during which price inflation will once again accelerate leading to a more serious recession in only a few years, and if this is accompanied by food shortages around the world, what might the prospects be within nations and among nations for not only economic stability but inter- national political harmony? (17)

Similarly, the unplanned but assured outcome of cultural dom- ination that once derived matter-of-factly from control of the flow of capital and access to the informational apparatus that it guaranteed can no longer be taken for granted. Accordingly, de- liberate management of the sphere of consciousness has become necessary. And it has been undertaken for some time, along with the customary, commercial, "unintentional" domination that characterized the preceding era. Conspiracy need not be invoked to demonstrate that there is a large measure of inten- tion in contemporary, American, cultural domination.

Consider, for example, the nature and direction of communi- cations research in the United States. Its interests parallel and undergird the corporate system that finances most of it. Com- munications research, while retaining its concern with audi- ences and the stimuli that excite them (the commercial compo- nent of the field), has become internationalized, better to serve its chief sponsor, the MNC. Hamid Mowlana (18) offers rich documentation about this development. He writes: "In the last decade (1960-1970), the comparative and integrated study of

social institutions, political behavior, social change, public
opinion and mass media has received unprecedented emphasis
by the United States scholar" (p. 79). Though Mowlana's study
of research on international communications encompasses a
span of 120 years, beginning in 1850, he finds, not surprisingly,
that "More than half of the studies coded — 52 per cent — were
written between 1960 and 1969" (p. 81). Also, as might be expected, "Studies in specific cultural and geographical areas
have corresponded roughly to United States involvement in those
areas." Mowlana adds, "This factor of involvement seems to
have influenced heavily what domestic studies have been undertaken and what foreign works translated" (p. 82). He concludes,
without further elaboration, that "United States interests and
involvements in world events generate scholarly studies as
much as methodological and research developments" (p. 90).

Otherwise stated, American corporate enterprise stimulates
and promotes the research studies and methodologies that it requires for its maintenance and expansion. And, in fact, an entirely new subdivision of communications study has arisen to
focus in a concentrated way on these matters. Happily named
"public diplomacy," the area is described by a university center of public diplomacy (19) as concerning itself with "the cause
and effect of public attitudes and opinions which influence the
formulation and execution of foreign policies" (p. 7). Another
way of saying this is that public diplomacy is actually the utilization of communications research and related interdisciplinary
fields for getting a grip on the minds of foreign audiences so
that the foreign policies of the United States or, for that matter,
any nation utilizing such techniques are admired, or at least
accepted and tolerated.

Some examples of public diplomacy in action are offered by
one of its scholars and practitioners. Glen H. Fisher (19), Dean
of the Center for Area and Country Studies in the Foreign Service Institute of the U.S. Department of State, writes: "...skill
must be used in choosing international actions in the first place
which can be expected to gain the desired objectives..." (p. 7).
For this reason Fisher believes that the space exploration pro-

gram contributed substantially to "American stature in the international arena." So, too, he says, "The Peace Corps certainly was conceived with an age of public diplomacy in mind" (p. 8). On the other hand, Fisher is concerned that although "The American public easily believed, after evidence was responsibly and carefully sifted, that President Kennedy's death was the murder act of one deranged person...a surprisingly widespread belief [existed] abroad that a plot had been swept under the rug" (p. 20).

Obviously, public diplomacy runs into difficulties when the events or programs cannot be managed entirely or staged by the public diplomats. But the objective is clear — however complicated and troublesome to achieve: "one must usually attempt to capture the mentality of significant groups"; and "a nation [must be understood] as a communication system" (p. 44).

These are challenging tasks for communications researchers, but scholars have not been reluctant to accept them. The U.S. Information Agency (USIA), a $200-million annual operation and a major employer of personnel with communication skills, operational and analytical, is in the forefront of the new praxis. Wilson P. Dizard (20), one of its most knowledgeable officials, writes: "As practitioners of the fragile art of presenting American attitudes and actions, we must now shape our operation in a much more sophisticated manner, with greater attention to the sensitivities of our audience than ever before." And "What USIA needs, first and foremost, is to improve its listening instruments, its sensitive intake channels." This plea for better communications research about international publics makes the additional point that "Our primary role in this effort is to sensitize policy makers, from the White House on down, in the relevance, and the specific details of the communications environment abroad."

The recent surge in research on international communications found by Mowlana, the appearance of the new field of public diplomacy described by Fisher, and the exhortation of USIA officials to "sensitize" policy makers to the international communications "environment" are different facets of the same

condition, i.e., the global involvement of U.S. capitalism and
its urgent need for reliable information about the climate of
opinion in the areas in which it is active.

Communications policy researchers, promoted from their
former limited but not inconsequential role as advisers to advertisers and public relations men, now stride in the corridors
of embassies and general staff headquarters. Their contribu-
tions are well understood and increasingly sought. The Shah of
Iran not only makes multibillion-dollar armament purchases
from the United States but also constructs a telecommunications
system linking 52 cities with the capital, Tehran. (21) The system, it can be assumed, will provide the infrastructure for both
physical control and cultural domination.

Foundations, private institutes, and university programs have
taken up the increasingly pressing issues of control of information in an unsettled and explosive international environment.
The rising level of attack in many places against the more manifest aspects of cultural domination requires informed and sophisticated responses from the dominators and their representatives. Forums such as UNESCO and the United Nations are
now the scenes of intense and critical debate on matters of cultural sovereignty and cultural imperialism. However unself-
conscious policy may have been in the past, now and for the future, acknowledgment of and deliberate preparatory action in
the ideational area are a growing feature of corporate capitalist
"planning." (22)

A privately supported but government-appointed panel on international information, education, and cultural relations, under
the chairmanship of Frank Stanton, one of the most influential
and official voices in the U.S. communications industry during
the last thirty years, explained the new role of communications
in the changed environment of the 1970s:

> While the United States retains considerable, perhaps
> predominant, power in international affairs, the capacity
> of America to dictate the course of international events
> has diminished. This means that the United States will

have to count more than ever on explanation and persuasion. The new premium on persuasion makes cultural
diplomacy essential to the achievement of American policy goals. (23)

Though it is certainly true that "the capacity of America to
dictate the course of international events has diminished," the
roots of "cultural diplomacy" extend back to a time when U.S.
corporate-military power was surging into the international
arena. It is to this period, in which the principles of communication control were first elaborated, that we now turn our attention.

2 THE DIPLOMACY OF CULTURAL DOMINATION AND THE FREE FLOW OF INFORMATION

"If I were to be granted one point of foreign policy
and no other, I would make it the free flow of information."

— John Foster Dulles

For a quarter of a century, one doctrine — the idea that
no barriers should prevent the flow of information among nations
— dominated international thinking about communications and
cultural relations. The genesis and extension of the free flow of
information concept are roughly coterminous with the brief and
hectic interval of U.S. global hegemony, an epoch already on the
wane. As we look back, it is now evident that the historical coincidence of these two phenomena — the policy of free flow of
information and the imperial ascendancy of the United States —
was not fortuitous. The first element was one of a very few indispensable prerequisites for the latter. Their interaction deserves examination.

As the Second World War drew to a close, attention in the
United States at the highest decision-making levels was already
focusing on the era ahead. In 1943, two years before the war's
end, it was clear that the United States would emerge from the
conflict physically unscathed and economically overpowering.

In the most general terms, the more articulate exponents of
what seemed to be a looming American Century envisioned a
world unshackled from former colonial ties and generally accessible to the initiatives and undertakings of American private
enterprise. Accumulated advantages, not all of them war related, ineluctably would permit American business to flourish
and expand into the farthest reaches of the world capitalist system. The limits that the very existence of a sphere under

24

socialist organization put on this expansion were, it might be
noted, neither agreeable nor acceptable, at that time, to a self-
confident North American leadership.

The outward thrust of U.S. corporate enterprise was economic, but the utility of the cultural-informational component
in the expansion process was appreciated at a very early stage
in the drama. The rapid international advances of U.S. capitalism, already under way in the early 1940s, were legitimized as
unexceptional and highly beneficial expressions of growing freedom in the international arena — freedom for capital, resources,
and information flows.

It was an especially propitious time to extol the virtues of unrestricted movement of information and resources. The depre-
dations of the Nazi occupation had traumatized Europe and a
good part of the rest of the world. Freedom of information and
movement were the highly desirable and legitimate aspirations
of occupied nations and peoples. And it was relatively easy to
confuse truly national needs with private business objectives.

John Knight (1), owner of a major chain of newspapers in the
United States, and in 1946 the president of the American Society
of Newspaper Editors, made a point, which left out more than it
explained, that many were expressing at the time: "Had not the
Nazi and Fascist forces in Germany and Italy seized and dominated the press and all communication facilities at the start,
the growth of these poisonous dictatorships might well have
been prevented and the indoctrination of national thought in the
direction of hatred and mistrust might have been impossible."

Free flow of information could not only be contrasted to the
fascist mode of operations but also was associated with the hope
for peace shared by war-weary peoples everywhere. Palmer
Hoyt (2), another influential American publisher, declared a few
months after the war's end:

> I believe entirely that the world cannot stand another
> war. But I believe as completely that the world is headed
> for such a war and destruction unless immediate steps
> are taken to insure the beginning at least of freedom of

news — <u>American style</u> — between the peoples of the
earth. A civilization that is not informed cannot be free
and a world that is not free cannot endure. [Emphasis
added.]

U.S. advocates of ease of movement of information then cap-
italized heavily on the experiences and emotions of people
freshly liberated from fascist-occupied and war-ravaged continents. But accompanying the rhetoric of freedom were powerful economic forces employing a skillful political and semantic
strategy.

In the first decades of the twentieth century, important sectors of domestic industry chafed impatiently at being excluded
from vast regions preempted by the still-forceful British and
French empires, i.e., the British global imperial preferences
that tied together that colonial system's network of dependencies and sealed them off from possible commercial penetration
by other entrepreneurs. The decisive role played by the British
worldwide communications network — both its control of the
physical hardware of oceanic cables and its administrative and
business organization of news and information — which held the
colonial system together, promoted its advantages, and insulated
it from external assault, had not escaped attention in the United
States. It was against these finely spun, structural ties that an
American offensive was mounted. Conveniently, the attack
could avail itself of the virtuous language and praiseworthy objectives of "free flow of information" and "worldwide access
to news."

But there was no mistaking the underlying thrust. For years
Kent Cooper, executive manager of the Associated Press (AP),
had sought to break the international grip of the European news
cartels — Reuters, foremost, and Havas and Wolff. Cooper's
book <u>Barriers Down</u> (New York, Farrar and Rinehart, 1942) described the global territorial divisions the cartels had organized and the limitations they posed for the activities of the AP.
As early as 1914, Cooper wrote, the AP "board was debating
whether the Associated Press should not make an effort to

break through the Havas (French) control of the vast South
American territory" (p. 41). He recalled, "The tenacious hold
that a nineteenth century territorial allotment for news dissemination had upon the world was evidenced by each year's discussion of the subject by the Associated Press Board of Directors,
continuing until 1934" (p. 43).

Cooper's indictment of the old cartels has an ironic quality
today when U.S. news agencies largely dominate the flow of
world information:

> In precluding the Associated Press from disseminating
> news abroad, Reuters and Havas served three purposes:
> (1) they kept out Associated Press competition; (2) they
> were free to present American news disparagingly to the
> United States if they presented it at all; (3) they could
> present news of their own countries most favorably and
> without it being contradicted. Their own countries were
> always glorified. This was done by reporting great ad-
> vances at home in English and French civilizations, the
> benefits of which would, of course, be bestowed on the
> world. (P. 43)

Cooper also recognized the significance of Britain's domination of the oceanic cables:

> The cable brought Australia, South Africa, India, China,
> Canada and all the British world instantaneously to Lon-
> don on the Thames.... Britain, far ahead of any other
> nation, concentrated on the cable business. First it tied
> its Empire together. Then it stretched out and tied other
> nations to it. And in harmony with Victorian practices,
> the news that went through this vast network of cables
> gave luster to the British cause! (P. 11)

Cooper was not alone in seeing these advantages. James Lawrence Fly (3), chairman of the Federal Communications Commission during the Second World War, also drew attention to this subject:

Among the artificial restraints to the free development
of commerce throughout the world none is more irksome
and less justifiable than the control of communication facilities by one country with preferential services and
rates to its own nationals....

Great Britain owns the major portion of the cables of
the world, and it is a fair statement that, through such
ownership and the interlocking contractual relations based
on it, that country dominates the world cable situation.
(P. 168)

This understanding of the power afforded by domination of communications was not forgotten. It was manifest two decades
later when U.S. companies, with huge government subsidies,
were the first to develop and then monopolize satellite communications.

The impatient U.S. press associations and governmental communications regulators found others in the country who recognized the advantages that worldwide communications control
bestowed on foreign trade and export markets. Business Week
(4) reported:

...Washington recognizes the postwar importance of
freer communications as a stimulant to the interchange
of goods and ideas. On a less lofty level it means that
federal officials are trying to loosen the grip which the
British have long held through their cable system, which
they tightened after the last war through the seizure of
German properties.... In peacetime, reduced costs of
messages will energize our trade, support our propaganda, bolster business for all the lines.

The magazine summed up the business view by quoting approvingly a comment that had appeared in the London Standard: " 'It
[control of communications] gives power to survey the trade of
the world and...to facilitate those activities which are to the
interest of those in control.' "

Of course, British power was not unaware of American interest in these matters. The influential Economist reacted tartly
to Kent Cooper's expanding campaign, in late 1944, for the free
flow of information: The " 'huge financial resources of the American agencies might enable them to dominate the world....
[Cooper], like most big business executives, experiences a peculiar moral glow in finding that his idea of freedom coincides
with his commercial advantage.... Democracy does not necessarily mean making the whole world safe for the AP.'" (5) Nor
did it mean, the Economist failed to add, retaining control for
Reuters and British Cables.

The public official most directly concerned with formulating
and explaining U.S. policy in the communications sphere immediately after the war was William Benton, the Assistant Secretary of State. Benton (6), who was to become a U.S. Senator and
president of the Encyclopedia Britannica, outlined, in a State
Department broadcast in January 1946, the government's position on the meaning of freedom of communications:

> The State Department plans to do everything within its
> power along political or diplomatic lines to help break
> down the artificial barriers to the expansion of private
> American news agencies, magazines, motion pictures,
> and other media of communications throughout the
> world.... Freedom of the press — and freedom of ex-
> change of information generally — is an integral part of
> our foreign policy.

The economic aspects of the free-flow-of-information policy
certainly were no secret, though the media neither dwelt on the
self-serving nature of its widely proclaimed principle nor made
the implications of the policy explicit to the public. Instead, a
remarkable political campaign was organized by the big press
associations and publishers, with the support of industry in general, to elevate the issue of free flow of information to the highest level of national and international principle. This served a
handsome pair of objectives. It rallied public opinion to the

support of a commercial goal expressed as an ethical imperative. Simultaneously, it provided a highly effective ideological
club against the Soviet Union and its newly created neighboring
zone of anticapitalist influence.

It was obvious that the fundamental premise of free enterprise — access to capital governs access to message dissemination — would be intolerable to societies that had eliminated
private ownership of decisive forms of property, such as mass
communications facilities. Therefore, the issue of free flow of
information provided American policy managers with a powerful cultural argument for creating suspicion about an alternate
form of social organization. It thus helped to weaken the enormous popular interest in Europe and Asia at the war's end in one
or another variety of socialism.

John Foster Dulles, one of the chief architects and executors
of America's Cold War policy, was forthright on this matter:
"If I were to be granted one point of foreign policy and no other,
I would make it the free flow of information." (7) This is a re-
curring theme in postwar U.S. diplomacy. For example, a couple of years later, the U.S. delegation to a United Nations Conference on Freedom of Information (8) reported:

> It is the hope of the six of us that this Conference
> helped to turn the tide that has been running against free-
> dom throughout much of the world. It is our conviction
> that in the future conduct of our foreign policy the United
> States should continue to take vigorous action in this field
> of freedom of thought and expression.

Certainly the chronology of the launching and steadfast pur-
suance of the free-flow doctrine supports the belief that the issue had been thoughtfully prepared and carefully promoted in
the critical period immediately preceding the end of the Second
World War and the few years directly thereafter. Those who
select the interval beginning in 1948 as the start of the Cold
War era overlook the earlier period when the groundwork was
prepared in the United States for the general offensive of Amer-

ican capitalism throughout the world. This was the time, too,
as we shall see, when the free-flow question first came to
prominence.

Well before the war was over, American business had incorporated the issue of free flow of information into a formal political ideology. In June 1944 the directors of the powerful American Society of Newspaper Editors adopted resolutions urging
both major political parties to support "world freedom of information and unrestricted communications for news throughout
the world." (9) Thereupon, both the Democrats and the Republicans, in the next two months, adopted planks in their party platforms that incorporated these aims. The Democrats proclaimed:
"We believe that without loss of sovereignty, world development
and lasting peace are within humanity's grasp. They will come
with the greater enjoyment of those freedoms by the peoples of
the world, and with the freer flow among them of ideas and
goods." The Republicans stated: "All channels of news must be
kept open with equality of access to information at the source.
If agreement can be achieved with foreign nations to establish
the same principles, it will be a valuable contribution to future
peace." (10)
    In September 1944 both houses of Congress adopted a con-
current resolution that followed closely the recommendations
of the editors and publishers. Congress expressed "its belief
in the worldwide right of interchange of news by news-gathering
and distributing agencies, whether individual or associate, by
any means, without discrimination as to sources, distribution,
rates or charges; and that this right should be protected by international compact." (11)
    Having sought and secured congressional endorsement of their
aims, the directors of the American Society of Newspaper Editors, meeting in November 1944, then declared that "most Americans and their newspapers will support Government policies...
and action toward removal of all political, legal and economic
barriers to the media of information, and... our Government
should make this abundantly clear to other nations." (12) The

group noted with satisfaction that the newly appointed Secretary
of State, Edward Stettinius, Jr., had announced that "...the
United States plans exploratory talks with other nations looking
to international understandings guaranteeing there shall be no
barriers to interchange of information among all nations." (13)

At the same time, the American Society of Newspaper Editors, in conjunction with the AP and United Press International
(UPI), announced an international expedition of a delegation to
"personally carry the message of an international free press
into every friendly capital of the world." (14) In the spring of
1945, while the war was still being fought, the delegation trav-
eled 40,000 miles around the world, to twenty-two major cities
and eleven allied and neutral countries, "on first priority of the
War Department on Army Transport Command planes." (15)

While the private group of U.S. press representatives was
making its international journey to marshal support for the
free-flow doctrine, the directors of the Associated Press
"placed a fund of $1,000,000 a year at the disposal of Executive
Director Kent Cooper to make the AP a global institution." (16)

In fact, as the war drew to a close, preparations for the promotion of the free-flow doctrine shifted from the national to the
international level. With congressional and political support assured and domestic public opinion effectively organized, the
free-flow advocates carried their campaign vigorously into the
channels of international diplomacy and peacemaking that were
becoming activated with the end of hostilities.

One of the first occasions that provided an opportunity for an
international forum for espousing the free-flow doctrine was the
Inter-American Conference on Problems of War and Peace con-
vened in Mexico City in February 1945. Latin America, regarded for more than a century as a prime U.S. interest — with
European economic influence practically eliminated as a result
of the war — was a natural site for testing the new doctrine in
a congenial, if not controlled, international setting. Predictably, the conference adopted a strong resolution on "free access to information" that was "based substantially on a United
States proposal." (17)

The Western Hemisphere having been successfully persuaded of the merits of "free flow," attention turned to the rest of the world. International peacekeeping structures were being established; and the United States made certain that the newly created United Nations, and the related United Nations Educational, Scientific, and Cultural Organization (UNESCO), would put great emphasis on the free-flow issue.

The utilization of the United Nations and its affiliated organizations as instruments of U.S. policy and, additionally, as effective forums for the propagation of the free-flow doctrine can best be understood in the context of the international economy thirty years ago.

In the 1970s, the United States often is on the minority side of the voting in the United Nations (on some issues in almost total isolation — e.g., on direct satellite broadcasting). In the 1940s, affairs were quite different.

Fifty states were represented in the first meetings of the United Nations in 1945, hardly more than a third of the present 143-nation membership. Of the original 50, two-fifths were Latin American states, at that time almost totally subservient to North American pressure. The West European member states were economically drained, politically unstable, and heavily dependent on the United States for economic assistance. The few Middle Eastern, Asian, and African countries then participating in the UN were, with a few exceptions, still, in real terms, subject to the Western empire system. In sum, the United Nations, in 1945-48, was far from being universal, much less independent. In fact, it was distinguished by an "automatic majority," invoked whenever its heaviest financial supporter and economically strongest member desired to use it.

Western image-making and information manipulation often made a great play of Soviet obduracy, as reflected in its use of the veto. Unmentioned were the political and economic relationships that permitted decisions favorable to the United States to be voted routinely with overwhelming majorities. In this atmosphere the UN's endorsement of the free-flow doctrine was hardly surprising. It was also poor evidence that the principle had genuinely international support or that its full import was appreciated. Rather, it offered a striking example of how the machinery of international organization could be put at the disposal of its most powerful participant. What follows is a very brief review of the utilization of UNESCO and the United Nations itself for the propagation of the free-flow doctrine.

The earliest proposals for the constitution of UNESCO, which were drafted by a U.S. panel of experts and reviewed by the State Department, prominently espoused the free flow of information as a UNESCO objective. (18) In an account of the meetings of the U.S. delegation to the constitutional conference of UNESCO in Washington and London in October and November 1945, the head of the delegation, Archibald MacLeish, repeatedly emphasized his (and the delegation's) conviction that the free flow of information was a basic principle. (19) There is no reason to doubt this. Many people in the United States, especially in the literary and humanistic arts, fully supported the concept of free flow, unaware of, or perhaps indifferent to, the central purpose the doctrine served or to which it was meant to be applied.

It is in this respect that the first report of the United States National Commission for UNESCO (an appointed group, heavily representative of the cultural arts) to the Secretary of State (20), in early 1947, is an unusual document. It contained a mildly worded qualification with respect to the free-flow doctrine. The commission recommended:

> The American Delegation [to UNESCO] should advance and support proposals for the removal of obstacles to the free flow of information in accordance with the report of the Committee of Consultants to the Department of State on Mass Media and UNESCO. The Commission differs, however, with the Committee of Consultants in believing that the organization should concern itself with the quality of international communication through the mass media and should give serious study to the means by which the mass media may be of more positive and creative service

to the cause of international understanding and therefore
of peace. [Emphasis added.]

The commission hastened to add, "The Organization should, of
course, avoid at all times any act or suggestion of censorship."

The concern for quality rarely, if ever, found its way into official U.S. pronouncements on the desirability of the free flow
of information. When suggested, as it regularly was by the state
ownership societies, it was rejected out of hand as a justification for censorship and suppression. When it was also raised
as a major consideration by the Hutchins Freedom of the Press
Commission in the United States in 1946, it was simply
ignored. (21)

From the start, UNESCO, with the U.S. delegation taking the
initiative, made free flow of information one of its major concerns. In its account of the first session of the General Conference of UNESCO, held in Paris in November-December 1946,
the U.S. delegation reported that it had proposed to the subcommission on mass communications that "UNESCO should co-
operate with the Subcommission on Freedom of Information of
the Commission on Human Rights in the preparation of the
United Nations report on obstacles to the free flow of information and ideas..." (22) In fact, a section on free flow of information was created in the Mass Communications Division of
UNESCO itself.

In the United Nations similar initiatives for stressing and
publicizing the free-flow doctrine were under way from the outset of that organization's existence. The United Nations Economic and Social Council established the Commission on Human
Rights in February 1946 and, in June 1946, empowered this commission to set up a subcommission on freedom of information
and the press. (23)

Earlier, the delegation of the Philippines Commonwealth had
addressed to the Preparatory Commission of the United Nations,
for submission to the first part of the first session of the UN's
General Assembly, a draft resolution that proposed an international conference on the press with a view "to ensuring the

establishment, operation, and circulation of a free press throughout the world." (24) With due respect to national sensibilities, it is impossible to imagine the Philippines' initiative, preceding the first General Assembly of the United Nations, without the support, if not encouragement and sponsorship, of the United States. The Philippines had been, since the end of the nineteenth century, and in a real sense still were in 1946, a dependency of the United States.

A new draft was introduced by the Philippines delegation to the General Assembly during the second part of its first session (October 15-December 1946). This proposed that the international conference be extended to include other informational media such as radio and film. On December 14, 1946, the General Assembly adopted Resolution 59(1), which declared that "freedom of information is a fundamental human right, and is a touchstone of all the freedoms to which the United Nations is consecrated," and that freedom "implies the right to gather, transmit and publish news anywhere and everywhere without fetters." (24) The Assembly also resolved to authorize the holding of a conference of all members of the United Nations on freedom of information.

The United Nations Conference on Freedom of Information was held March 25-April 21, 1948, in Geneva. It provided the international ideological polarization the United States' policy managers had expected of it. William Benton (25), chairman of the United States delegation to the conference, explained: "Our Conference at Geneva, as was to be expected [Emphasis added.], is sharply divided.... The free are thus face to face with those whose ideology drives them toward the destruction of freedom." But, Benton continued, "...we are not at Geneva to make propaganda. We are there to do all that we can to reduce barriers to the flow of information among men and nations." Yet among the main objectives of the American delegation, still according to Benton, and hardly compatible with his plea of nonpartisanship, was "...to secure agreement upon the establishment of continuing machinery in the United Nations that will keep world attention focused on the vital subject of freedom of expression within and among nations."

The conference's final act, embodying essentially U.S. views on free flow of information, was adopted by thirty votes to one (Poland's being the dissenting vote), with five abstentions (Belorussia, Czechoslovakia, the Ukraine, the USSR, and Yugoslavia). The Soviet proposal that the final act be signed only by the president and the executive secretary of the conference instead of representatives of all the attending governments did not please the U.S. delegation. Nevertheless, perhaps because of the uneasiness aroused by the conference's overtly provocative character, the Soviet recommendation was unanimously adopted. (26)

The conference voted also to refer the resolutions and its draft convention to the UN Economic and Social Council for consideration and eventual submission, for final adoption, to the General Assembly. In August 1948, after acrimonious and protracted debate, the Economic and Social Council submitted the entire parcel — three conventions and forty-three resolutions — without action or recommendation to the 1948 General Assembly, where it languished, without any action's being taken. (27) Despite the strong U.S. influence in the United Nations at the time, the organization's structure made it difficult to bulldoze all issues through the intricate web of committees, commissions, and the General Assembly.

The conference itself represented, in the eyes of U.S. observers, "in the main...a victory for American objectives.... Out of 45 substantive propositions, the [U.S.] delegation voted against only one, and abstained from voting on only three, thus supporting 41 decisions of the Conference." (28) Others saw it differently. The Economist (London), for example, though generally approving of the work of the conference, noted:

> ...it was the impression of most delegations that the Americans wanted to secure for their news agencies that general freedom of the market for the most efficient which has been the object of all their initiatives in commercial policy — that they regard freedom of information as an extension of the charter of the International Trade

Organization rather than as a special and important subject of its own. And the stern opposition which they offered to Indian and Chinese efforts to protect infant national news agencies confirmed this impression. (29)

This assessment by the Economist reflected the continuing
ambivalence of the United States' West European allies toward
the issue of free flow of information. Though fully cognizant of
the commercial threat the free-flow doctrine posed to their own
communications industries, faced with the United States' media
power, the Western market economies, especially Great Britain,
nonetheless supported the principle as a means of embarrassing
the Soviet sphere and placing it on an ideological defensive. On
this question a united Western position defending private ownership of the mass media took precedence over the internal conflicts in the Western world about who should dominate these instruments.

Though efforts to gain wide international support for the free-
flow concept were at best inconclusive, the two decades following the Freedom of Information Conference in 1948 saw the realization of the doctrine in fact, if not in solemn covenant. New
communications technology — computers, space satellites, television — combined with a powerful and expanding corporate
business system, assisted the push of the United States into the
center of the world economy.

Without public pronouncements, private, American-made media products and U.S. informational networks blanketed the
world. Especially prominent were films, produced more and
more frequently outside the country (30); the exportation of
commercial television programs (31); and international distribution of North American magazines and other periodicals.
Reader's Digest, Time, Newsweek, Playboy, and Walt Disney
Corporation productions reached millions of viewers and read-
ers outside the United States. Moreover, foreign book-publishing
firms disappeared into U.S. "leisure time" conglomerates.
Along with these more or less conventional media penetrations,

a variety of additional informational activities accompanied the global surge of private American capital. Foremost, perhaps, was the extension of the opinion poll and consumer survey, now undertaken all over the world, often under the auspices of American-owned research companies. (32)

Largely as a reaction to the flood of American cultural material and the usurpation of national media systems that were required to disseminate it, a new mood with respect to the doctrine of free flow of information became observable in the international community in the late 1960s and early 1970s. Besides the free-flow view, one began to see frequent references to cultural sovereignty, cultural privacy, cultural autonomy, and even admissions of the possibility of cultural imperialism. (33)

Another factor that perhaps is contributing to the shift of emphasis, outside the United States, away from the quantity to the consequences of free flow of information is the changed nature of the international community itself. Since 1945 more than ninety new national entities, most of them still in an early stage of economic development, have emerged to take their places in the community of nations. A paramount concern of these states is to safeguard their national and cultural sovereignty. Then, too, the results of two decades of de facto free flow of information have not gone unremarked. It is difficult, in fact, to escape the global spread of U.S. cultural styles featured in the mass media of films, TV programs, pop records, and slick magazines. Their influence prompts sentiments such as that expressed by the Prime Minister of Guyana: "A nation whose mass media are dominated from the outside is not a nation." (33)

Twenty-five years later, the 1948 comments of Robert D. Leigh (34), director of the staff of the Hutchins Commission on Freedom of the Press, have a prophetic ring:

> The main burden of my presentation is that in the present day, and especially across national boundaries, this faith in an omnicompetent world citizen served only by full flow of words and images is an oversimplification of the process and effect of mass communication....

"Barriers Down" standing by itself is not adequate policy
in the international field. The focus changes from free
individual expression as a right, to the primary need of
the citizen everywhere to have regular access to reliable
information, and, also, ready access to the existent diversity of ideas, opinions, insights, and arguments regarding
public affairs. This does not deny freedom, but it joins
freedom with a positive responsibility that freedom shall
serve truth and understanding. The concept of responsibility, carried to its logical conclusion, may even imply
defining a clearly harmful class of public communication
which falls outside the protection of freedom itself.
(P. 382) [Emphasis added in last sentence.]

Finally, the possibility of direct satellite broadcasting from
space into home sets without the mediation of nationally controlled ground stations, whether or not likely in the immediate
future, has created a sense of urgency concerning the question
of cultural sovereignty. This has been especially observable in
the United Nations.

The Working Group on Direct Broadcast Satellites was established in 1969 "to consider mainly the technical feasibility of
direct broadcasting from satellites." (35) It has met more or
less regularly since that time, extending its range from the
technical aspects to the social, legal, and political implications
of direct, satellite broadcasting.

Moreover, UNESCO, the strongest advocate of the free-flow
doctrine at one time, has veered noticeably away from its formerly unquestioning support. In its Declaration of Guiding Principles on the Use of Satellite Broadcasting for the Free Flow of
Information, adopted in October 1972, UNESCO acknowledged
that "...it is necessary that States, taking into account the principle of freedom of information, reach or promote prior agree-
ments concerning direct satellite broadcasting to the population
of countries other than the country of origin of the transmission." (36) The UN General Assembly supported this view in
November 1972, by a vote of 102 to 1 — the United States

casting the single dissenting vote.

Reactions in the private communications sector in the United States were predictably hostile and self-serving. Frank Stanton (37), one of the most influential American media controllers in the era of U.S. informational hegemony, wrote: "...the rights of Americans to speak to whomever they please, when they please, are [being] bartered away." His chief objection to the UNESCO document, he claimed, was that censorship was being imposed by provisions that permitted each nation to reach prior agreement with transmitting nations concerning the character of the broadcasts.

Stanton, along with a good part of the media's managers (including the prestigious New York Times), finds the right of nations to control the character of the messages transmitted into their territories both dangerous and a gross violation of the U.S. Constitution's provision concerning freedom of speech: "The rights which form the framework of our Constitution, the principles asserted in the Universal Declaration of Human Rights, the basic principle of the free movement of ideas, are thus ignored." (37)

Along with the hubris displayed in regarding the U.S. Constitution applicable to, and binding law for, the entire international community is a second, even more questionable, consideration. Stanton and those in agreement with him matter-of-factly assume that the United States' constitutional guarantee of freedom of speech to the individual is applicable to the multinational corporations and media conglomerates whose interests they so strongly espouse. Yet more than a generation ago, Earl L. Vance (38) asked, "Is freedom of the press to be conceived as a personal right appertaining to all citizens, as undoubtedly the Founding Fathers conceived it; or as a property right appertaining to the ownership of newspapers and other publications, as we have come to think of it largely today?"

Stanton et al. extend the property-right concept of freedom of speech to all the advanced electronic forms of communication and expect universal acquiescence in their interpretation. But the national power behind this view is no longer as absolute or

as fearsome as it was in 1945. The world is no longer totally
dependent on, and therefore vulnerable to, the economic strength
of the United States. A remarkable renewal of economic activity
in Western Europe and Japan, significant growth and expansion
of the noncapitalist world, and, not least, the experiences of the
last quarter of a century have produced an altogether changed
international environment.

This new atmosphere, as we have noted, is reflected in the
voting patterns of international bodies — so much so, in fact,
that U.S. spokesmen complain bitterly that the United Nations
and UNESCO, in particular, are practicing a "tyranny of the
majority" that "brutally disregards the sensitivity of the minority." (39) Worse still, these organizations are being "politi-
cized." (40)

It is worth quoting the response of the Algerian delegate to
the United Nations to these charges. Abdellatif Rahal (41) re-
minded the Assembly:

> It may not be unimportant to begin by stressing that
> countries which today are rebelling against the rule of
> the majority are the very same which constituted the ma-
> jority of yesterday, the same whose behavior at that time
> represented the best frame of reference for judging the
> behavior of today's majority.... Thus, if those who now
> criticize us protest the very rules which govern our work
> in this Assembly, they should remember that they them-
> selves are the authors of these rules, let them not forget
> that the lessons they wish to give us today are worth little
> when compared with the examples they have already given
> us in the past.

To be sure, the United States and its closest allies (and com-
petitors) still emphasize the free-flow doctrine as the basis for
peace and international security. The Helsinki Conference on
Security and Cooperation in Europe, begun in mid-1973 and concluded in July 1975, made this very clear. In its preliminary
consultations the conference was instructed to "prepare pro-

posals to facilitate the freer and wider dissemination of information of all kinds." (42) And it was this issue to which the
Western delegates gave their greatest attention, seeking to make
all other decisions contingent on a resolution of the free-flow
question acceptable to themselves. British Foreign Secretary
Sir Alec Douglas-Home (43), for instance, declared:

> ...the item...on an agenda which deals with co-operation
> in the humanitarian field is in my judgment the most im-
> portant item of our business. If our Conference is essen-
> tially about people and about trust then it is necessary
> that we do something to remove the barriers which inhibit
> the movement of people and the exchange of information
> and ideas.

But despite the insistence of most of the political and economic leaders of Western, industrialized, market economies on
the continued importance of an unalloyed free-flow doctrine,
alternate formulations are appearing. One was contained in the
speech of Finland's President, Urho Kekkonen, before a communications symposium in May 1973. Kekkonen (44) in a comprehensive review of the fundamental premises of international
communications, singled out the free-flow doctrine for his scrutiny:

> When the Declaration of Human Rights was drawn up
> after the Second World War, the 19th century liberal
> view of the world in the spirit of the ideas of Adam Smith
> and John Stuart Mill was the guideline. Freedom of action
> and enterprise — laissez-faire — was made the supreme
> value in the world of business and ideology, irrespective
> of at whose expense success in this world was achieved.
> The State gave everyone the possibility to function, but
> did not carry the responsibility for the consequences. So
> the freedom of the strong led to success and the weak
> went under in spite of this so-called liberty. This was the
> result regardless of which of them advocated a more just
> policy for society and mankind.

Kekkonen applied this general perspective to international communication and the free-flow doctrine. He noted:

> In the world of communications, it can be observed how problems of freedom of speech within one State are identical to those in the world community formed by different States. At an international level are to be found the ideals of free communication and their actual distorted execution for the rich on the one hand and the poor on the other. Globally the flow of information between States — not least the material pumped out by television — is to a very great extent a one-way, unbalanced traffic, and in no way possesses the depth and range which the principles of freedom of speech require.

These observations led Kekkonen to inquire: "Could it be that the prophets who preach unhindered communication are not concerned with equality between nations, but are on the side of the stronger and wealthier?" He remarked also that international organizations were in fact moving away from their original advocacy of the free-flow doctrine:

> My observations would indicate that the United Nations and its educational, scientific and cultural organization, UNESCO, have in the last few years reduced their declarations on behalf of an abstract freedom of speech. Instead, they have moved in the direction of planing down the lack of balance in international communications.

From all this, Kekkonen concluded: "...a mere liberalistic freedom of communication is not in everyday reality a neutral idea, but a way in which an enterprise with many resources at its disposal has greater opportunities than weaker brethren to make its own hegemony accepted."

Kekkonen's analysis is, in fact, the general conclusion, however long overdue, that is beginning to emerge with respect to all international and domestic relationships — not just those

concerned with communications. When there is an uneven distribution of power among individuals or groups within nations
or among nations, a free hand — freedom to continue doing
what led to the existing condition — serves to strengthen the
already-powerful and weaken further the already-frail. Evidence of this abounds in all aspects of modern life — in race,
sex, and occupational and international relationships. Freedoms that are formally impressive may be substantively op-
pressive when they reinforce prevailing inequalities while
claiming to be providing generalized opportunity for all.

Not surprisingly, individuals, groups, and nations increasingly are seeking means to limit the freedom to maintain in-
equality. Measures aimed at regulating "the free flow of information" are best understood from this perspective. Moreover,
they explain new developments in U.S. cultural-communications
policy, which are the subject of the next chapter.

3 THE TECHNOLOGY
OF CULTURAL DOMINATION

After thirty years of almost unqualified acceptance (except by the Soviet sphere) in international politics, the doctrine of free flow of information is now increasingly on the defensive. The "final act" at Helsinki — the outcome of the 1973-75 Conference on European Security and Cooperation — contrary to official American pronouncements, may be interpreted as a definite limitation on the free-flow concept. (1) Similarly, the 18th General Conference of UNESCO, in the fall of 1974, approved a medium-term plan for 1977-82 which suggested that the traditional notion of the free flow of information "needs to be complemented by that of a more balanced and objective flow, both between countries and within and between regions." (2)

Not without reason, therefore, are decision-makers and advisers intensifying their search for policy alternatives that will permit a continued U.S. influence, if not dominance, in international cultural and economic affairs. More often than not, the alternative emphasized and encouraged is technology. In fact, the present design of U.S. cultural policy seems to be to rush advanced communications technology into place and into operation. This technology embraces computer networks and satellite broadcasting systems, all of which can operate transnationally.

For example, Leonard Marks (3), a former director of the United States Information Agency, addressing a conference sponsored by the U.S. State Department in 1974, is quite explicit:

...Our strategy cannot be based on the current communications system.... Long before a direct broadcast satellite becomes feasible, however, there will be global electronic networks — some of which are already in operation — which will pose realistic questions about information flow and cultural integrity.... These networks will
move massive amounts of information through high-speed
circuits across national boundaries. Moreover, they will
be effectively beyond the reach of the traditional forms
of censorship and control. The only way to "censor" an
electronic network moving...648 million bits per second
is literally to pull the plug. The international extension
of electronic mail transmission, data-packet networks
and information-bank retrieval systems in future years
will have considerably more effect on national cultures
than any direct broadcast systems. Our strategy will
have to take this into consideration. (P. 66)

Mr. Marks also sounds a note of urgency and regards with ap-
prehension efforts to limit the introduction of the new technology: "In the short run, however, our problem is preventing pre-
cipitate action toward imposing international restrictions on
any communication technology" (p. 68).
    The strategy is well founded. The offer of advanced technol-
ogy, communications technology especially, cannot fail to be
alluring to a large part of the international community. For
this reason alone it is imperative today to consider the general
role of technology not only as an instrument for effectuating
cultural domination but as an embodiment of this very domination.

    The present world is sharply divided between industrialized,
relatively well-off societies and nonindustrialized, impover-
ished peoples. The attraction of economic development has an
understandably powerful, perhaps irresistible, appeal to poor
countries and their leaders. The conditions accompanying development along Western lines are less appreciated.

Technology and the way it is used affect the basic infrastructure of social communication. Thus the acceptance of a
"developmentalist strategy" in a nation introduces more than
industrial techniques and equipment. The way human beings are
related to each other in work and in their community and family
life is largely, if not overwhelmingly, determined by the nature
of the technology employed, how it is employed, and the social
relations that govern its use. It is paradoxical, but perhaps inevitable, that the discussion of development in Western literature inverts the relationships and confuses initiating with re-
acting forces. This is particularly noticeable with respect to
the interaction of development with communications.

A substantial literature, the bulk of which appeared in the
United States, as might be expected, in the brief ascendancy of
American international power after the Second World War, has
linked communications — the mass media in particular — closely
with economic development. The central assumptions are based
on the influential role mass communications can play, through
exhortation and imitation, in instructing "traditional" people to
follow the ways of the more advanced societies. Thus, proponents of these views suggest the desirability of having the modern media promote "empathy" for change, for becoming "modern," for discarding "traditionalism," for desiring the goods of
Western consumer society, for leaving the countryside and mi-
grating to the city and becoming "urbanized."

A group of political scientists at the Massachusetts Institute
of Technology, of whom Daniel Lerner, Frederick Frey, Ithiel
de Sola Pool, and Lucian Pye are most prominent, are associated
with one, or another, or all of these conceptions. Lerner's
theory of communications and development, perhaps the most
comprehensively elaborated, is described by Frey (4), "...at
the core, the theory describes the process of modernization in
terms of four variables: urbanization, literacy, mass media exposure and 'participation.'..." And, further, "everywhere...
increasing urbanization has tended to raise literacy; rising literacy has tended to increase media exposure; increasing media
exposure has 'gone with' wider economic participation (per

capita income) and political participation (voting)."

At about the same time that Lerner was elaborating this theory of development dependent on communications, UNESCO,
still firmly a U.S. international adjunct (see the previous essay)
was publishing criteria for minimally desirable levels of media
adequacy for development. These were the familiar ratios of
newspaper consumption, radio sets, cinema seats, etc., per
capita. (5)

Yet the sequence is backward. Though it is undeniable that
the mass media, following Western prescriptions, produce will-
ing participants for a developmental course patterned on the
Western model, the relationship is an after-the-fact one. First
comes the system itself, however it emerges or is introduced
into the "traditional" organism/society. The process that Western academics call "modernization" generally follows the introduction of the business system, its commercial arrangements,
financial networks, economic activities, and, not least, its technological structures and processes. It is all of these, in toto,
that initiate and require the modernization campaigns. And it
is the technology — broadly defined as organizational structures, administrative hierarchies, and, of course, equipment
and processes — that determines the fundamental communications patterns.

The mass media — the press, radio, television — supplement
and extend the message the system wants conveyed. But the basic substructure of material productive arrangements induces
and compels the message's formulation and character. This occurs, to be sure, somewhat mysteriously, to everyone concerned. Technology as we have defined it and the conditions of
productive life are seen as normal, natural, and nonideological.
This is especially observable with respect to "hard" technology.

Technology, which appears mainly, and is almost exclusively
understood, as visible machinery and hardware, lends itself
admirably to the claim that it is neutral, value free, and em-
ployable under any social order, for sometimes quite different
ends. Moreover, the concept of free flow of information, which
holds that benefits accrue to everyone participating in that flow,

but which, in reality, is a one-way street for exercising domination by the already-powerful, is extended to technology — with
the still greater likelihood of intensifying the dependency of the
weaker parties. (6)

It is important to recognize that the technology of advanced
capitalism is hardly likely to be appropriate for developing
countries, and it is essential to understand that this technology
is in itself an expression of the capitalistic structures and the
strivings from which it emerged. The conceptions and designs
for the hardware and the processes that accompany it are
shaped by, and come out of, the production and social relations
existing at the time.

Certainly, the development of technology — in contrast to in-
ventive ideas that do not materialize — depends entirely on its
acceptance by, and encouragement from, the decision-making
power centers of the economy. It would be inconceivable for
this to be otherwise. As Nicholas Garnham (7) puts it,

> ...we should see technology rather as those potentialities
> which a particular social power structure chooses to con-
> cretize and institutionalize.... In short, questions of the
> relationship of a technology to a society are political
> questions. They concern the power relations within the
> society and value judgments as to the shape of that soci-
> ety, the direction of its development, and the utilization
> of resources to that end.

Raymond Williams (8) explains that one of the continuing con-
fusions is the belief that "new technologies are invented as it
were in an independent sphere, and then create new societies
or new human conditions." The historical reality is different.
Williams notes:

> In no way is this [television and related electronic devel-
> opments] a history of communications systems creating
> a new society or new social conditions. The decisive and
> earlier transformation of industrial production, and its

new social forms, which had grown out of a long history
of capital accumulation and working technical improve-
ments, created new needs but also new possibilities, and
the communications systems, down to television, were
their intrinsic outcome.

Technology is a social construct and serves the prevailing
system of social power, though it often contributes to changes
in the organization and distribution of that power. In Western
European and North American economic development, private
ownership of productive resources has provided the base of
that social power. The technology that has been developed arose
out of the felt needs of that power and has been utilized to con-
solidate and extend it. The interaction of technology and capitalism and the presentation of that inseparable interrelationship
as apolitical deserve the closest scrutiny.

Dallas Smythe (9) insists that the idea that "technology is autonomous" is itself "a political concept." To accept "technology
as a universal tendency (or an autonomous factor) inevitably
leads people to regard technology as something that is happening to them without their consent, awareness or the possibility
of controlling it."

The belief that productive forces evolve autonomously may
have been appropriate to an earlier historical time; but at least
since the Second World War, massive governmental and corporate budgets have been allocated to scientific and technological
research with deliberate objectives in view. The technical applications that derive from these enormous expenditures can
hardly be regarded as having been randomly discovered or autonomously developed.

Inability to recognize the social origins of technology explains, in large part, the sense of individual helplessness that
pervades most advanced industrialized states today. Yet in the
important fields of communication and transport the evidence
of the capitalistic origins and system-determined nature of the
technology in use is overwhelming.

Radio and television broadcasting, for example, as Williams

observes, were organized and developed in the context of an already-atomized society, each fragmented family unit living in its private home. And this arrangement was the inevitable outcome of a market-dominated development that broke up the community and sealed individuals into isolated physical and psychological cubicles. Transmission from centralized message centers to atomized individual receivers serves and replicates the one-way flow that is built into the system and that separates the rulers from the ruled.

So, too, the automobile, as Garnham (10) writes,

> ...was not the product of the invention of the internal combustion engine, but the internal combustion engine was rather one of the instrumentalities sought and found by capitalism at a certain stage of industrial development to be put into social use through the development of production-line techniques and, even more important, marketing. The automobile industry, as we know it, moreover, depended for its growth on inserting these instrumentalities into a political structure which bore the burden of road-building publicly while allowing the profits of automobile manufacture and sale to be accumulated privately.

The ecological crisis that hangs over industrial society provides the ultimate evidence. Barry Commoner (11) has carefully traced some of the relationships that reveal the connection between the prevailing technology and the social system. He states:

> The crucial link between pollution and profits appears to be modern technology, which is both the main source of recent increases in productivity — and therefore of profits — and of recent assaults on the environment. Driven by an inherent tendency to maximize profits, modern private enterprise has seized upon those massive technological innovations that promise to gratify this need, usually unaware that these innovations are often instruments of environmental destruction.

The basic factor in the introduction of new technology is obviously the quest for profitability. The "unawareness" of the consequences is actually an indifference to the social costs — the ensuing environmental degradation — that affect society, not the producer.

What is of special interest here is Commoner's finding that the technology, introduced in the United States especially since the Second World War, has demonstrated an overwhelming tendency to degrade the ecosystem. But, as we know, this vital information is presented to the general public by the system-serving informational apparatus in a totally vitiated form. The relatively mysterious abstraction "technology" is offered to the people as an explanation for rampaging ills — not the specific technology of profit-seeking capitalism.

One of the most striking and continuing examples of how science, technology, and "objectivity" are directed comes from the military sphere, Pentagon financing having dominated research in the United States for more than a generation. On the basis of a study of Department of Defense contracts at Stanford University active on February 9, 1971, two scientists (12) found:

> Our study demonstrated that the military had developed a rational, well-administered program to define research priorities in terms of current and projected military needs and to purchase R&D from universities based on these needs. Thus, while the scientific process as reflected in each individual project proceeded objectively, funding availability biased scientists' choices on which projects to pursue. (P. 706) [Emphasis added.]

These scientists quote Department of Defense officials:

> "The DOD [Department of Defense] is not simply accepting scientific and technological products coming from a random pattern of independent research activities in the universities. Rather DOD interest in some particular area can stimulate growth and development planned to fill

specific short-term and/or general long-term technological gaps in the military's capability." (P. 710)

Another example of the sociopolitical origins of technology is
provided by the circumstances surrounding the development of
communications satellites. Though the technology has been
praised for its capability to provide global instruction, cultural
enrichment, and instantaneous accessibility to informational
storehouses throughout the world, it is necessary to remember
that the research and development funds that led to the concep-
tion and production of these high-flying transmitters and anten-
nae were provided by an American military-commercial alli-
ance with very clear objectives in mind. This was no random
search for improved means of communication. Satellite development, from the beginning, represented the successful drive
of private communications corporations in the United States to
dislodge the British from their domination of international communication, exercised through their (British) control of inter-
continental submarine cables. In this effort monopolistic business worked closely with the U.S. Armed Forces, whose interest in instantaneous global communications was extraordinarily
high — as well it might be, with the task of servicing an American empire with troops deployed on all continents. In fact, the
first communications satellite system in operation was a
military-controlled operation. (13)
    A decade later, in the early 1970s, an international consor-
tium (called INTELSAT) of (currently) 91 nations uses the United
States-developed satellite system. The system has, from the start,
been controlled by American Big Business — A.T.&T., I.T.T.,
RCA, Comsat — working intimately with the U.S. State Department
at the intergovernmental level. (14) In recent years nationalistic
impulses among many members of INTELSAT have forced a
diminution in formal control by the United States (through the
voting mechanism). Nevertheless, all the participants have accepted the principles and operating procedures of a technical
system organized by private business monopolies, with market
standards explicit in its structure and criteria of rationality.

A chronicler of INTELSAT (14) reports approvingly that
"...decisions [can] be made in terms of financial or technical
objectives regardless of political goals or long-term ideals"
(p. 158). In other words, the 91 member countries of INTELSAT,
its entire membership, including Yugoslavia and several Third
World nations, have approved, to date, the supremacy of the
principles of efficiency and functionalism above political and
social considerations. This is no small ideological and profit-
producing victory for capitalism in general and American corporate business in particular. For when the market definition
of "efficiency" is applied, the likelihood, even the possibility,
of including social factors in the calculation of costs or benefits inevitably disappears.

To sum up: technology — communication technology especially — has been, certainly since the end of the Second World
War, and still is, conceived, developed, and saturated with the
interest and specifications of monopoly capitalism. The possibility of alternate uses, in some cases, of a technology, whatever its origins, must be admitted. But this is a subject for
careful evaluation on a case-by-case basis. More will be said
about this in what follows.

Inasmuch as Western technology not only is an integral part
of an exploitative system of production but extends and deepens
that exploitation, is an alternative conceivable?

One possible approach is to reject the prevailing features of
Western technology while examining possible alternative directions that technological discovery might have taken if the moti-
vations and incentives and distribution of social power had been
different. Basic to this view is the recognition that inventions,
discovery, and science in general evolve out of the historical
process and from the socially experienced needs of an age. In
the development of this or that process or product or machine,
there are alternatives and different opportunities. The distribution of social influence and authority determines what course
and which option will be followed, which opportunities will be
seized and which left unexplored.

Garnham (15) notes, for example, how the Luddite movement in England, at the time of industrial capitalism's early development, has been maligned and its challenge deliberately misinterpreted:

> Until recently this movement of opposition to nascent industrial capitalism by a nascent working class, has been characterized as stupid, doomed opposition to beneficent progress. It was no such thing. It was rather a struggle not about technology itself (the weavers wanted relief from backbreaking toil), but about choices of technologies and the uses to which technology was to be put. . . . They [the Luddites] were against the introduction of a technology that favoured centralized control by capital in factories over decentralized control by the weavers themselves.

Though many of the initial opportunities for a different historical course may have been irrevocably lost, recognition that what in fact now prevails is evidence neither of its evolutionary superiority nor of its inevitability is extremely important in itself — particularly for societies that may still have some measure of choice. (16) Certainly understanding that the adoption of a technology will have a far-reaching and possibly destructive influence on an entire web of social relationships is an elemental precondition for meaningful social decision-making.

The least that could be expected from such an understanding is a deceleration in the rush to copy and follow Western developmental (and communications) models. This suggests resistance to the view that development is a "race," that participation in the race cannot be delayed, and that the race must be run on the track already prepared by those who have been traveling dizzily around its course for a long time.

The standing order with respect to importing Western technology into the Third World and elsewhere might be "Why rush?" Indeed, the watchwords might better be delay, postpone, defer. John Lent (17) asks, for example, about a situation "such as in

Malaysia where plans are moving ahead for color television
before black and white has been fully implemented. Why?" The
answer comes not exclusively from Malaysia but also from the
center of monopoly capitalism. The market for black and white
sets in the United States in the late 1950s was nearly saturated.
To keep production moving and profits high, color television
was rushed onto the domestic market and expensively promoted.
Did Americans need this? Do Asians benefit from following the
same course?

Evidence from a variety of sources suggests the enormous
utility of deliberation, reflection, careful evaluation, and hesi-
tancy before introducing anywhere the latest models of advanced
technique and research coming out of the corporate, profit-
oriented West.

For example, the implications and the effects of the highly
publicized Green Revolution — the introduction of high-yielding
varieties of seeds to many Asian countries — are only now beginning to be considered. According to a report in Science magazine (18):

> An important general criticism of the Green Revolution is
> that, far from being custom-designed for less developed
> countries, it is simply American agricultural technology
> transferred abroad. The most pressing aspect of this
> criticism is that the Green Revolution package, like Amer-
> ican agriculture, is reliant on high energy inputs such as
> fertilizer, pesticides, and fuel.... Green Revolution crops
> perform to meet the Western commercial criteria of large
> production and high profits. They are bred and designed
> to be grown as monocultures and in monocrops, the whole
> field being planted to the same single variety of the same
> crop.... Reduction of diversity is generally only of ad-
> vantage in a highly commercialized agriculture, where
> crop uniformity is an aid to mechanized harvesting, pack-
> aging and marketing. For the peasant farmer, reduction
> in the number of crops or varieties he plants is a guaran-
> tee only of greater risks.

What is offered as life-saving technology may instead be a
community-shattering disaster.

Another grim example of what may be expected of market-
spawned technology comes from the medical field. Cancer specialists point out that "Cancers we are now seeing had their
origins 15 to 35 years ago... The air we breathe contains
gases and particles that never before entered the human lung.
Our food has chemicals designed to improve its taste, fresh-
ness and appearance — but which are strange to our intestines,
livers, kidneys, blood." They further note that "There has been
and continues to be no pre-testing of materials for cancer or
other serious disease. Examination is for serviceability, sale-
ability, utility." (19)

Not long ago a group of American molecular biologists recommended that certain kinds of genetic engineering experiments
be discontinued until the risks inherent in such work could be
ascertained. A science writer (20) commented on this unprecedented suggestion, "...we have no really useful mechanisms
for sensible prior discussion of issues like these in scientific
research.... We need, urgently, to develop better social and
political mechanisms for anticipating dangerous research and
probably for controlling it, too."

On the same question of "human engineering," an American
scientist, Leon Kass (21), wrote movingly:

> Because we lack wisdom, caution is our urgent need. Or
> to put it another way, in the absence of that "ultimate wis-
> dom," we can be wise enough to know that we are not wise
> enough. When we lack sufficient wisdom to do, wisdom
> consists in not doing. Caution, restraint, delay, absten-
> tion are what this second-best (and perhaps only) wisdom
> dictates with respect to the technology for human engi-
> neering. [Emphasis added.]

He asks, "Is there not something contradictory in the notion
that we have the power to control all the untoward consequences
of a technology, but lack the power to determine whether it

should be developed in the first place?" (p. 786).

These are physical questions. Who has begun to think of the cultural-psychological questions, of the effects on the hearts and minds of hundreds of millions of people of the receipt of messages tested only for advertising impact and consumerist efficacy?

Only a few people in already-developed market societies, forced by intensifying social crisis into reflection, are timidly expressing the need for caution and restraint with respect to science and technology. Still fewer are making the connection between the nature of the research and technology and the structure of the prevailing socioeconomic order. Nevertheless, with respect to agriculture, medicine, atomic energy, electric power production, synthetic detergents, and a growing number of industries and products, the sentiment is developing that it is time — past time — to call at least a temporary halt.

Whether this is even feasible in a solidly entrenched market system is open to question. The point here, however, is that uncertainty and doubt have arisen in the center of the global capitalist structure itself about the work of that system. Surely the yellow light of caution should be flashing throughout the periphery of the system — in all those dependent, semidependent, and half-allied states that constitute the grotesquely named "free" world. In the noncapitalist orbit as well, nations that have covertly or openly been fascinated by Western techniques and models might begin to reassess their infatuations.

There are no simple rules or guidelines that can be offered to those concerned with avoiding the calamitous course that the private-propertied societies now appear to be following. Certainly understanding the social basis of the origins and forms of technology is obligatory. The extent to which a social structure reflects the interests of its working population may be the clue to a nation's vulnerability to the imposition of a repressive technology. Where the social system makes no pretense about its class character, the consequences are clear: further absorption into the Western economic and value system is inevitable.

It is doubtful whether an independent national policy is even

partially attainable in a class-stratified society founded on
property and privilege. Surely, the same or similar imperatives, e.g., pacifying the working people, organizing consumer-
ism, catering to middle-class strivings for status, and, above
all, maintaining the system, are present in all market societies — developed, developing, and still to develop. It is therefore likely to be simply a matter of the degree, related to the
developmental level, of the imitation, penetration, and domination that occur in any peripheral or semiperipheral market-
structured economy.

Nevertheless, it may still be useful to describe briefly a few
general approaches toward technological autonomy that may be
applicable, at least in societies with a socialistic base.

If we begin with the recognition that technology and its allied
processes originate in the systemic needs of the dominating
class, it follows that peripheral, weak, and dependent nations
are never considered, insofar as their genuine needs are concerned, by the producers and exporters of new technology. A
couple of statistics are instructive: Mowlana (22) has observed
that "Ninety-eight per cent of the scientific and technological
research at present is being undertaken in the advanced industrial states — drawn on their own experiences. Only one per
cent of the research is directed at the special problems of developing countries."

The space program is a dramatic example of a technology
serving existing power but promising rich benefits to the power-
less. A New York Times report (23) noted that "the United Nations itself has neither the technical manpower nor finances to
assist [poorer] countries to utilize the new discoveries. Currently, the space program has a $77,000 annual budget that is
supposed to cover the costs of acquainting 100 countries with
all aspects of space application." By way of comparison, the
United States' space agency, NASA, annually had approximately
$5 billion at its disposal over a 15-year period, and in 1975
still disposed of $3.5 billion.

Is it surprising, then, that the weaker states must take what
the dominators offer? But if the dominated cannot trust, much

less rely on, the good services and instrumentation of their powerful sources of supply, what can they do? In brief, they can rely on themselves. This is the only way weak states can be assured that they will not be in a condition of perpetual dependence on their "benefactors."

What are some of the elements of a policy of self-reliance? One perspective, presupposing a society in which capitalism has been largely, if not entirely, eliminated and some basic features of socialism installed, gives highest priority to central planning and strict controls over economic life — arrangements that would strongly influence the flow of technology. These arrangements would regulate the composition of imports and exports, the amount (if any) of foreign investment, the level and nature of personal consumption (including the consumption of information), and, not least, the control and limitation of tourism and similar activities that distort the structure and behavior of the economy and the people. Such self-reliance

> ...would involve the use of the resources of the nation for the satisfaction of the three socialist values: essentials, employment, and equality. Resources would no longer be wasted on the consumption of Western, luxury gadgets by a small minority group. They would, instead, be devoted to the production and distribution of food, health care, housing, and schools for everybody. (24)

These priorities permit other, important benefits to accrue. They automatically provide a breathing space, a pause, before rushing into ill-judged or unassessed transfers or applications of technology of more advantage to investing foreign enterprises than to local living. In addition, they allow selectivity to become a basic operating mechanism for evaluating what may be useful in the spectrum of process and product ostentatiously displayed, or vigorously hawked, in the technologically metastasized West. The cautionary words of Frantz Fanon (25) are applicable to all potential emulators of the Western developmental model:

...We today can do everything so long as we do not imi-
tate Europe, so long as we are not obsessed by the desire
to catch up with Europe.... Two centuries ago, a former
European colony decided to catch up with Europe. It suc-
ceeded so well that the United States of America became
a monster in which the taints, the sickness and the in-
humanity of Europe have grown to appalling dimensions....

No, we do not want to catch up with anyone. What we
want to do is to go forward all the time, night and day, in
the company of Man, in the company of men. The caravan
should not be stretched out, for in that case each line will
hardly see those who precede it... We must turn over a
new leaf, we must work out new concepts, and try to set
afoot a new man.

Is selectivity in picking and choosing for local application the
processes and products of the monopoly capitalist countries a
feasible option? The most that can be said at this point is "perhaps." But even "perhaps" may be too generous an appraisal
if a clear overview does not accompany the selection process.
In such an overview the national community and its leadership
must work out in advance a prospect for man and woman, the
place of human beings in the economy and the basic goals of the
community itself. Dallas Smythe (26), who has given considerable thought to these matters, has observed, "There is no socialist road in Western capitalist technological development."
The reality is that there is no shopping center available in
which neutral machinery, processes, and goods are displayed
for the convenience and choice of prospective participants in
the development "race." What is offered can in no way be regarded as what is needed. If there is such a correspondence,
it is accidental. It can and should be taken advantage of. But
reason suggests that such lucky mutualism can be only an in-
frequent coincidence. This is noted by Alisjahbana (27):

...the question of whether or not appropriate, intermedi-
ate technology or an alternative technology is available

for LDCs [less developed countries] should not be made
dependent on the question of whether that technology is
available in the world or foreign market. It is the LDCs'
thinkers and LDCs' research institutions as one of the
elements in its chain of development that should decide
this question, with the help of all progressive think[ers
and] potentials of the developed world.

But in truth it is the lack of competent and skilled assessing institutions and individuals that poses the problem to begin with.
If dependency in the technological area were not so absolute,
the dangers would be far less and the alternatives more easily
imagined.
    Juan Corradi has called attention to the feeble and dependent
condition of science and the scientific community in Latin America, for example. It is another facet of the general state of dependency and exploitation. Corradi (28) describes what he terms
"scientism" and its consequences for South American nations:

    In more concrete terms, "scientism" refers today to
    the condition of those Latin American scientists who are
    adapted to the international scientific market — itself
    dominated by highly developed branches of knowledge —
    and who have abandoned the concern for the social and
    cultural implications of their activities in the context of
    Latin American dependence. They devote their efforts to
    specialized research, accepting the goals and standards
    established by international centers. Some important con-
    sequences follow from this situation. One of them is that
    scientism reinforces cultural and other forms of depen-
    dence in Latin America. The situation of dependence finds
    expression both in the internal development of scientific
    research and organization in each country, and also in the
    international "brain drain" from dependent to metropoli-
    tan areas. "Scientistic" scientists in Latin American
    countries tend to become perpetually frustrated. Those
    devoted to basic research and who aspire to enter the

higher circles of international scientific communities are
often frustrated by innumerable institutional and cultural
obstacles in their countries: from outright suspicion or
lack of official encouragement to absence of funds and
equipment as well as permanent insecurity. In seeking to
escape these frustrations, many develop intimate ties
with foreign institutions operating abroad or in situ, the
priorities of which are by no means consonant with the
best interests of Latin American countries. Other scientists have lowered their standards and have become gatherers of data for processing elsewhere or else apply lo-
cally the results of research done elsewhere. They tend
to be more thoroughly "deintellectualized" than basic researchers, in the sense of being specialized scientific
workers. The intellectual predicament is strikingly parallel to the economic constellation of dependence: Latin
American countries become producers of raw data and
exporters of qualified scientific personnel. (Pp. 48-49)

Is it reasonable to expect that this situation can produce the
kind of selectivity in technological matters that is required to
overcome dependency? Hardly! Even less may be expected
from the advanced capitalist centers of development. There,
whatever assessment there is, has been traditionally undertaken by the same groups and interests that control the research and the products that research stimulates. Actually, instead of assessment, there is often an effort, in the United
States at least, to prevent the consideration of the possible
long-term effects of a new technology. The case of direct satellite broadcasting is illustrative.

Though no one has claimed that transmitting from a space
satellite into a home receiver is immediately in prospect, the
technology is known and capable of construction. Consequently,
it is not surprising or alarmist that many nations have expressed a deep concern about the possible results of direct satellite broadcasting some time in the future. This concern is an
outgrowth of the existing state of affairs, in which a handful of

media conglomerates in the rich, industrialized, capitalist economies already dominate the international flow of news, films,
magazines, TV programs, and other items.

Efforts undertaken in UNESCO and the United Nations to fore-
stall the complete capture of direct satellite broadcasting by
these same commercial interests are bitterly contested by the
United States. (29) The United States' position, directly expressing the interests of North American media conglomerates, has
been that "any international agreement on the principles that
should govern satellite broadcasting [is] premature." According to this view (29)

> ...the immediate task [is] not to develop the principles
> of an international agreement but to experiment with sat-
> ellite broadcasting so that its full potential may ultimately
> be achieved and to develop the spirit and methods of in-
> ternational cooperation in this field. If rules were pro-
> mulgated too soon, said the United States, they might
> freeze the development of satellite broadcasting. (P. 11)
> [Emphasis added.]

In short, no rules, no assessment; let the technology prolif-
erate. Only after it has created its own imperatives, according
to the prevailing corporate power structure in which it develops, is the subject of regulation and control legitimate. Then,
of course, the pattern has been set; and the rule-makers are
faced with technological and economic faits accomplis.

Edwin Parker (30) has reflected on the problems confronting
those who wish to see "constructive" and "progressive" applications of technology. He writes:

> ...the core of the problem lies in the social institutions
> that control the development and deployment of technol-
> ogy... The institutions that have captured or grown up
> around the significant technologies of our time constitute
> the dominant order of society. Changing our technology
> of ground transportation [for example] will involve

changing the automobile industry and its suppliers (including the steel industry), the oil industry, and the self-
perpetuating dedicated gasoline tax system that supports
the continuing cycle of high construction at the expense
of other forms of transportation.

Parker concludes that before there can be assessment of technology in advanced capitalism, there must be a "change in social institutions."

In brief, serious assessment of technology is rendered impossible by the sheath of social institutions that currently support and dominate research and development. However, the
mounting environmental crisis in the United States is beginning
to provoke concern about the necessity for such assessment —
an assessment that might well challenge the basic structural
nature of the economy. For example, Ruth Davis (31), the director of the Institute for Computer Sciences and Technology
of the National Bureau of Standards, has written:

> However, it now seems quite clear that public patience
> with the cure always following after the ill has worn thin.
> The public wants to see some preventive measures taken.
> Indeed, individuals have taken what can be called preven-
> tive technology into their own hands. We have seen the
> public in action in this way in its handling of the super-
> sonic transport issue and its reaction toward siting of
> nuclear power plants. This is the reactive mode of prac-
> ticing preventive technology, and it hinges on public rec-
> ognition that technology is fallible. But it is important in
> practicing preventive technology to also recognize that
> science has been the primary cause of beneficial change
> throughout man's history.
>   It is now time for the formalization of preventive tech-
> nology as a scientific specialty. This new field must be
> populated with economists, lawyers, technologists, and
> scientists. It will be practiced during the entire cycle of
> research, innovation, application, diffusion, and impact

of technology. It will make possible both more science
and more public peace of mind and may already have
more focus than technology assessment or science policy.
It is safe to predict that delays in setting up preventive
technology as a scientific specialty bode ill both for science and for future beneficial changes for society.

Countries that have set out on new paths — those that have
already changed their basic social institutions — may hardly be
in a position to judge, in technical terms, the impact of sophisticated technology and processes developed in the West; but they
can assess the social structure of the system that is their pro-
genitor. Moreover, they, better than anyone else, can understand the needs of their own people; and they should have a vision of what their social objectives are.

These are very general tools indeed for policy making that
must deal with high-precision and complicated instrumentation.
The main point, it may be useful to repeat, is that despite the
urgency of vast, unmet, human need, caution is imperative. A
course of development that may be irreversible and that may
lead, at best, to a poor imitation of what already exists and
functions so disastrously, from a human standpoint, in the advanced capitalist part of the world is no benefit to the people
who desperately require material improvement. And, as we observed at the beginning of this discussion, the technology itself
is a powerful form of communication, not merely its channel
for transmission.

4 NATIONAL COMMUNICATIONS POLICIES: A NEW ARENA FOR SOCIAL STRUGGLE

Modern mind management, employing information, imagery, education, and technology, poses new problems to dominated people — both inside the core, industrialized countries and in the peripheral, dependent regions.

Class conflict historically has been seen as an economic battle, a conflict between contending groups, the working class against the property-owning class: in the near term, for a larger share of the immediate (annual) product; ultimately, for the control and direction of the productive system. Now, however, in the major, industrialized, capitalist nations of Western Europe, in North America and Japan, a new element has entered the confrontation: utilization to the hilt by the dominating class of an enormously expanded and totally penetrative informational apparatus. In the still-unindustrialized countries, struggling to overcome their economic dependency, national independence and social transformation are blocked to the extent that the communications system is controlled by or represents the dominating class, externally or internally based.

Accordingly, class conflict has now moved into the communications-cultural sphere in an explicit way; and the emergence of national communications policies is the reflection of generally still-unresolved battles between contradictory interests and demands in the cultural-informational sector. Yet this is no secondary level of conflict. The communications-cultural component has been enjoying a continuous expansion in

all market economies. It seems likely to become, both absolutely (in terms of workers employed, capital invested, value
of output, etc.) (1) and qualitatively (in terms of decisive influence), a critical, if not the central, locus of the future struggle
within and against capitalism. Examples of growing class and
national concern with the forces that create and shape individual
and group beliefs and outlooks are numerous and multiplying.

— The Finnish Government announced, in June 1972, the formation of an official committee to "consider the initiatives
which the State should take on problems of mass communication." (2)

— "Proposals for a Communications Policy for Canada" were
submitted by the government to public consideration in March
1973. And, in January 1975, the Secretary of State for External
Affairs declared a new policy for Canada, one that would
strengthen "the economy and other aspects of national life in
order to secure independence." (3)

— UNESCO's Advisory Panel on Communication Research
recommended, in 1972, the creation of national communications
policies. (4) In implementation of its panel's recommendation,
UNESCO supported a series of studies on national communications policies, which began to be published in 1974. (5) Earlier,
an Intergovernmental Conference on Cultural Policies in Europe, under UNESCO sponsorship, was held in Helsinki, in June
1972.

— European communications policies were the subject of a
symposium under the auspices of the International Broadcast
Institute in May 1973. (6) The Council of Europe, also, has begun to examine systematically the matter of European-wide
communications policies. (7)

— The British Labour Party (8), the common program of the
French Socialist and Communist Parties (9), the Peruvian Military Government, and the French Government have each, within
the very recent past, drafted more or less detailed programs
for national policies regarding communication and information.
In addition, a Colombian conference on communications policy (10) and the resolutions against cultural imperialism

adopted by the nonaligned (Third World) nations in Algiers in 1973 (11) reveal the international breadth of the concern.

As the communications-informational issue is inseparable from the ultimate issue of societal control, it is to be expected that claims to participate in communications policy making are not limited to official governmental ministers and agencies. Political parties, professional organizations, trade unions, academic institutes, international associations, and individuals as well are actively offering their views.

Obviously, the widening preoccupation with the communications-cultural condition springs from many and often divergent sources. Self-realization, working people's economic improvement, and national independence constitute some of the bases for concern, but other interests are also at work. Command of the economy by either newly emergent or long-existent propertied groups and the control of the cultural apparatus for the perpetuation of economic domination are also powerful considerations in the spreading emphasis on national communications policies.

It is to a closer examination of these different and contradictory currents that we now turn.

The struggle to overcome domination — external, where the power resides outside the national community; internal, where the power is exercised by a domestic ruling stratum — is the central, if not always recognized, issue in contemporary communications policy making. Internationally, nationally, and individually, the struggle, though often obscured, is between the forces of domination and those that resist and challenge that domination. All basic issues in communications today relate to this fundamental and increasingly intense confrontation.

The battlelines sometimes seem more clearly drawn in the international field because there they follow closely the more familiar contours of the developed/developing, rich/poor, white/colored, state power relationships. The colonial system, disappearing rapidly as a formal apparatus of domination, lives on and flourishes in an intricate web of economic, political, and cultural dependencies.

In the words of the leaders of the self-designated nonaligned
countries:

> It is an established fact that the activity of imperialism
> is not limited to political and economic domains but that
> it encompasses social and cultural areas as well, impos-
> ing thereby a foreign ideological domination on the peo-
> ples of the developing world. [Consequently], the heads-
> of-state and government of the non-aligned countries em-
> phasize the necessity of reaffirming the national cultural
> identity and of eliminating the destructive consequences
> of the colonial era and that they preserve their national
> culture and traditions. (11)

The maiming cultural aftereffects of imperialism would be
cause enough for preoccupation with communications-cultural
matters in the formerly colonial world. But it is not a question
of past relationships. Current patterns of domination persist —
some in new forms, many in familiar modes. For the new nations which were colonies not so long ago, the effort to create
communications-cultural policies for national liberation and to
satisfy the working people's needs for better material conditions
of existence is no marginal item.

Political change that does not radically affect the conditions
of people at the base of the social pyramid hardly deserves to
be called liberation. Liberation, when indeed it does occur, demands the recognition and the satisfaction of indigenous mass
needs.

For nations that were not held in the colonial grip, but for a
variety of reasons experience increasing cultural domination,
the issues of social integrity and survival are also deeply felt.
Canada, for example, a nation of enormous breadth and potential,
with a history of independence and development, now exhibits a
profound and justifiable concern with preserving its own culture
and retaining the opportunity to develop it further. Of the five
basic questions to which a governmental position paper in 1973
on national communications policy was addressed, three were

concerned with the issue of external domination.

The document, at its outset, asked: "How can Canadian tele-communications systems be developed and used, to the greatest possible extent, to foster Canadian social and cultural values, and to provide a sure means of disseminating a Canadian per-ception of Canada and of the world to all Canadians?" Also, "How can the east/west links, which are essential to the social, cultural, and economic development of the country, be main-tained and developed in relation to the powerful pull of north [Canadian]/south [United States] ties?" And, finally, "What can be done to ensure that Canadian communications systems are and remain effectively in Canadian ownership or under Canadian control?" (12)

External domination in cultural communications is achieved in many ways, but the essential prerequisite is the control of both the message (image, information) production and the mes-sage transmission channels. In two of the most important me-dia, film and television, the preeminent role of a few Western, industrial, capitalist states has been well documented.

Guback (13) has studied the mechanisms of U.S. private con-trol over both the financing and the distribution of films world-wide. "In any respect," he writes, "American distributors con-stitute the single most important group in Europe, if not around the world. In fact, in Europe, the largest film companies are not actually British or French or Italian or German — nor even European. They are American." On the production side, U.S. dominance is no less evident: "In 1969 American companies abroad made investments in 185 features produced at an esti-mated cost of almost $235 million (as against 142 films made in America for $228 million)."

Reflecting on this situation, Guback inquires: "In view of the massive American investment in Europe generally, and consid-ering the extent to which American companies finance and dis-tribute European films in particular — quite aside from U.S. films' domination of theatre screens — in what terms can one talk realistically about cultural identity?" This is precisely the question that is being raised around the world.

The television program production and distribution business is equally dominated by the United States and a few other Western countries. Nordenstreng and Varis (14) have documented this in their aptly titled study Television Traffic — A One-Way Street ?.

Underpinning all the media and communications systems in general is the technological base. The creation of new technology, its management, and its distribution are the ultimate tests of modern power and the ability to dominate. As might be expected, the United States, on the strength of its tremendous industrial base and twenty-five years of stupendous military research and development expenditures, enjoys a commanding position in this vital area. To be sure, this dominance is observed with satisfaction:

Technology is the leading source of increased productivity and efficiency, and its transfer has important consequences for international economic relations. The United States has for many years held leadership in research and its application for commercial purposes. It has also been the source of much of the managerial and marketing know-how moving into the world economy. (15)

In 1973, the royalties and fees collected by U.S. business for making available some of its processes and technology (by no means all, or any portion of it that assures continued paramountcy) amounted to $3.5 billion.

In the light of this heavy, in some instances almost total, dependency on foreign media products, foreign technology, and technical processes, the anxiety of developed and developing countries alike to preserve a modicum of cultural autonomy is quite understandable.

Yet despite the prevailing patterns of international media flows and the technical processes and economic power that support them, the technology now appearing could be disturbing, at least potentially, to the structure of domination that presently exists. Foremost in this respect is the surge of communications innovation that has appeared in the last few decades: television, satellites, cable, computers, etc.

It is realistic to imagine that this proliferation of improved and varied communication channels causes dislocation, problems, and even crises in established arrangements and accustomed modes of information and message handling. Indeed, the belief that technology alone is the source of modern man's unsettled state is a widely held view, especially in the United States. One writer, for example, reflecting on the increased interest in what he terms "policy research in mass communications" — what is referred to here as national communications policy making — attributes this interest mostly to "the exponential growth in the rate of technological change." He notes the accelerating rate of innovation in communication means (speech, 500,000 years; writing, 4,000 years; printing, 500 years; telephone, 100 years; radio, 50 years; television, 25 years; computers, 25 years; satellites, 10 years; etc.) and sees this as the prime mover in creating the social disturbances that are attracting attention to the communications sector of social existence. (16)

Some of this is no doubt true, but it misses the main point. To begin with, as Raymond Williams (17) has explained so well, technological change in and of itself is not the determining factor:

> In no way is this a history of communications systems creating a new society or new social conditions. The decisive and earlier transformation of industrial production, and its new social forms, which had grown out of a long history of capital accumulation and working technical improvements, created new needs but also new possibilities, and the communications systems, down to television, were their intrinsic outcome.

Technological innovation does not arise out of thin air. It is encouraged (or discouraged) by the prevailing social system and, moreover, is integrated into that system, usually to achieve the objectives of the dominant elements already commanding the social scene. Williams observes that often the innovations produce unexpected and even unassimilable effects that run counter to the expectations of the system's controllers. Never-theless, in the initial period of technical innovation, it is rea-sonable to assume that the new instrumentation will be seized and directed by the forces then controlling the community. But, of course, there will be all sorts of tugs and pulls; and out-comes are not always predictable.

What is apparent now in the United States and in other coun-tries in the midst of sweeping technological innovation in com-munications is an intensification of the struggle for domination, which is taking place on several levels. Foremost is the rivalry between the established owners of existing communication facil-ities and new investors in the new technology. Often, obviously, there is an overlap between these groups. For example, broad-cast moguls try to buy into cable facilities. Still, groupings, re-flecting ownership in the different modes of communication, are present and push their varying interests actively.

Another side of the conflict concerns the national and inter-national communities, though here, too, there are overlap and blurring. In satellite communications, for example, U.S. corpo-rate interests have wrested a good part of international commu-nications circuitry away from formerly dominant British private ownership. A similar situation exists in the computer industry, in which American corporate control is dominant in Europe. In both instances, with regard to satellites and to computers, there are joint ventures and sometimes common fronts organized by capital, flowing internationally, against the interests of working people in the countries involved. But it is not entirely a one-way street. The mass of the population, aware of the afore-mentioned battles, begins to assert its own claim, however mod-estly in the initial period, to participation in the control of the new instrumentation.

The outcome of the conflict is made somewhat (though not very much) more chancy because some of the patterns of sta-bility are temporarily disrupted. This is not to suggest, either,

that the entire system of control is momentarily nullified, or
that the technology is outside the conflict. Power-wielders retain the inside track, and the technology is incorporated (or
sometimes excluded) as much and as quickly as possible into
their special needs and interests. However, there is a glimpse
of new possibilities and other social arrangements — inside the
nation or completely external to the country — that may reveal
unexpected opportunities for asserting a claim to authority.

The case of satellite communications is illustrative. Conceived, researched, and created by the most aggressive core
of American capitalism, satellites have been organized into a
global system serving the objectives of American equipment
producers, electronics corporations, the military establishment,
and the general advertising and commercial community. At the
same time, the advent of space communications has spotlighted
the overall issues of structural control, financial and technological dependency, and the dramatic side of information penetration from the heavens. International recognition of these issues
has raised the struggle to escape domination to new levels. In
doing so it has attracted additional voices and diverse interests.
In this sense, the introduction of the new technology of space
communications has contributed to the ongoing efforts of those
in control to impose new and extraordinarily effective means of
domination. But it has also helped to arouse those who are now
dominated to increase their efforts at resistance and to extend
the area of conflict to a more visible arena.

Examination of the conditions in which cable television and
cassettes and computers are being introduced in the United
States and other Western nations reveals similar tendencies.
The dominating corporate interests administer the rules, set
the specifications, and largely determine the pace of introduction and the utilization of the new techniques and hardware. Yet
conflicts develop within the dominant industrial groups; and, as
a consequence, important and hitherto excluded publics sometimes force themselves into the decision-making. The discussion that is opened up, however reluctantly on the corporate
side, permits additional possibilities for challenges and

alternate models of application and use.

It is, then, the largely but not entirely successful effort of the dominating stratum to introduce and regulate the new technology for its own objectives (profit-making and system maintenance) that ignites and illuminates the discussion and debate in the society-at-large. Increased interest in national communications-cultural policy making is best understood from this perspective.

The existing pattern of unequal and unilateral information flows and the discoveries in communication technology are specifically identifiable factors that partly explain the increasing efforts in many countries to formulate national communications policies. Less visible but not less significant is the result of a long-term historical process that is still unfolding.

Enormous concentrations of private capital have assisted in the creation of large-scale industry, which in turn has provided a remarkably high level of productivity. The capability to manufacture greater and greater outputs with declining inputs of labor arises from the introduction of automated machinery, efficiency at the work site, and, not least, the efforts of a skilled and well-trained labor force.

As a consequence of the higher productivity in industry and of pressure from labor, one can now observe a substantial and enlarging portion of nonworking time in the daily lives of working people. Whether these nonworking hours deserve to be regarded as "leisure" or, probably more appropriately, as recuperative time from alienating labor is a matter that will not be taken up here. Nevertheless, in 1966 adults had, on the average, slightly more than five hours a day of what the government defines as "leisure," a significant portion of which was spent viewing television (one and a half hours daily). (18)

The combination of high productivity and great industrial capacity, along with a trained industrial labor force enjoying increased time away from work, contains all the instabilities, economic and nonmaterial, that threaten at any time to throw advanced capitalism into unprecedented economic and social crisis.

The system depends on continued, yet socially unplanned, expansion to keep its industry operating and the working force employed. The workers, until recently at least, shared rising material benefits and experienced a generation or more of relative job security. How inclined the workers may be to tolerate any serious setback through unemployment and industrial slump is a very uncertain matter. Moreover, a broadened stratum of well-educated, professional, managerial, and service workers adds an additional ingredient of potential instability to the ongoing order.

The old coercions of economic crisis, unemployment, hunger, and insecurity, though far from banished, are scarcely viable instruments for keeping a recalcitrant labor force in line, for damping down inflation, or for permitting the system to pause and reorganize its diverse and irreconcilable components.

These realities of contemporary industrial life make conscious reliance on persuasion and image creation a major and growing feature of modern capitalism. The annual revenue of the advertising industry in the United States in 1975 was expected to exceed $28 billion. Most of this huge outlay is absorbed in organizing and channeling consumer demand. The various social indicators do not offer information on other forms of psychological massage that now occupy a privileged place in the processes of government and industrial enterprise. Governmental information, industrial public relations, opinion polling, and mass media outputs in general are the present-day components of the systemic effort to cajole, persuade, manipulate, and govern.

Given these characteristics of late twentieth-century capitalism, it is not surprising that the formulation of national communications policy has a domestic as well as an international side. And the criterion of domination is equally applicable overseas and at home. Abroad, American corporations and their indigenous counterparts seek markets and operating security by gaining control of the infrastructure of persuasion — the mass media. Domestically, the process is essentially the same, but more advanced.

Inside the United States, communications issues of access,
regulation, utilization of the new technology, and financial support are seen best within the framework of an advanced and
crisis-riddled state capitalist order. The issues in communications assume increasing significance in the larger struggle to
maintain or to change the total system. Information and the entire communication process have become key elements in the
business of social control. Accordingly, national communications policy making may be regarded as a battleground of the
contending forces on the social stage.

For a time, it is possible that national communications policy
making may be exclusively in the domain of the dominating stratum, though the policies elaborated may reflect divisions of interest and opinion in that stratum as well. As recognition of the
significance of the informational sector develops and its role
becomes more fully apparent, it is inevitable that struggles to
participate in policy formulation will involve, more and more,
the attention of the dominated stratum.

It is to be expected that the workers most directly engaged in
the message-production system would be drawn into the question of national communications policy making. This occurs for
both material and nonmaterial reasons.

One of the basic characteristics of the message-making and
-transmission industry, the consciousness-shaping industry, is
precisely that it is an industry. In a market society, the media
in all their aspects conform to the economic imperatives that
affect other industries. Workers produce the values that owners
appropriate. One enterprise expands at the expense of another.
Concentration of media power follows an economic course and
is subject to the same constraints, or lack of them, as other
sectors of industry.

In the area of manufactured culture and information, direct
economic pressures are experienced by the labor force (journalists, photographers, broadcasters, reporters, copywriters,
editors, etc.). In the case of newspapers, for example, a trend,
observable in all advanced capitalist countries, for the press to

become tightly concentrated results in a heavy burden for the working force. As papers merge and staffs are consolidated, press workers lose their jobs.

When papers are bought and sold and new owners set different editorial policies, the employees are confronted with the hard fact of what freedom of the press means in a private-ownership context. It is this understanding, born of job and editorial insecurity, that produces a strong reaction among informed professional labor against the organizational arrangements that presently administer this sector of work. The movement for editorial democratization/participation in the Netherlands, for instance, is described as the direct outgrowth of economic crisis in the publishing industry. (19) A Federal Republic of Germany "fair" press bill has similar antecedents. (20)

It is noteworthy that it is material need in the consciousness-shaping industry — a sector that specializes in nonmaterial products — that forces attention to the larger issues of communications policy making and media control. But when the pressure of personal economic adversity is combined with an acknowledged high level of information that characterizes the working force in this area, some unusual patterns of resistance may be expected. In any case, the concern of workers in the consciousness-shaping industry at this time, especially those in the print field, for their material welfare brings an influential stratum of advanced capitalism's labor force into the emerging clash over communications policy making.

The struggle for a comprehensive approach to communications-informational affairs, one that strives actually to inform people, can in no way be regarded as an indication that in market economies no communications/cultural policy exists. To the contrary, a UNESCO panel of consultants (21) noted, in 1973: "Communications policies already exist in every society, though they may frequently be latent and disjointed rather than clearly articulated and harmonized. What is proposed is therefore not something radically new, but rather a new look, an explicit statement and a deliberately prospective reformulation of practices already generally established."

What exists, for the most part, in advanced market economies is a varying mixture of governmental regulation and sub-
sidization of the mass media. The government itself constitutes
a powerful news-generating agency. Beyond it is a more or less
freewheeling private sector that dominates communication activities outside the official sector. In this sector are included
film-making, TV production, newspapers, books, records, advertising, public relations, opinion polling, and market research.

In the private sector no policy as such can be said to prevail,
in that a prescribed set of rules and codes is generally absent.
There is rather what might be called institutionalized communications domination — much as the expression has been used
with respect to race and sex. Institutional racism, for instance,
argues that people are subject not to specific legislative acts of
discrimination, though these may be present too, but that social
existence is so structured that racism is inevitable. If blacks,
for example, have been excluded in the past from adequate education, the dynamics of the system operate to perpetuate the existing imbalances in income and opportunity. Individual components in the system may legitimately, if hypocritically, claim
that they are helpless to intervene because the disadvantaged
do not possess either the skills, training, personalities, etc.,
for the higher-paying work.

A parallel situation exists in institutionalized communications
domination. Again, a UNESCO report (22) describes the condition: "...the present media structures have grown from systems which were designed to affect a vertical information and
persuasion flow from the top to the bottom of society."

The from-the-top-down feature of communication flows is an
inevitable outgrowth of a class-structured system in which the
dominating class, the propertied stratum, sends down the
orders/information. Actually, communication facilities are regarded as property in most, if not all, market-organized economies. It is considered unexceptional that a private individual
or group can command a major channel of information. In this
arrangement it would be absurd to imagine that a message flow

relating to significant social decision-making could originate
at the bottom of the economy. There are times, and some of
these have been noted, when the dominated, the general public,
are solicited for their views. Invariably, this is not an aberra-
tion in the central mechanism, but a more refined means of
exercising a manipulative domination. (23)

To sum up: institutionalized communications domination in
market societies has, until recently at least, not required explicit rules/policies. The assumptions and the operative mechanics of a propertied system have permitted, more or less
unobtrusively, a communications flow that has served to reinforce the structure of domination based on property. Actually,
calling attention to the mechanics of this process might in itself have created problems for its beneficiaries. The system
worked best when it was regarded as unstructured and unar-
ranged.

The attention now being turned to the communications process
is the strongest indication of the growing struggle over communications domination. The description of a comprehensive Finnish effort to formulate a national communications policy supports this conclusion. Kaarle Nordenstreng (24), one of the
members of the Finnish policy drafting group, writes: "The
spirit of the suggested reform is rather for more rational co-
ordination and an increase in parliamentary influence (through
the Government) in the formulation of policies, and in making
politically important decisions more explicit" [Emphasis
added.].

When political (communications) decision-making is made
more explicit — and one can only take that to mean understandable to the public — the battleground becomes much more public as well. In place of either elite decisions by the controlling
few or a smoothly functioning, hegemonic system, the entire
area of decision becomes potentially a matter of intense popular discussion.

Naturally, this is not received with enthusiasm in all quarters. Although, as we have noted already, some agreement exists
that comprehensive or national communications/informational

policy is increasingly necessary, this developing consensus comes from opposite directions. Obviously, the different supporters of such policy making have different objectives.

The excluded sectors (working people, minorities, women) are moving toward making the process of information generation and transmission more open and available to public scrutiny and, most of all, more responsive to their needs. The advertisers, the corporations they serve, and a powerful sector of the governmental bureaucracy are moved by a different vision. For them the issue of policy formulation and research is to be approached carefully and narrowly. The assumptions underlying the communications system itself are not regarded as legitimate areas of inquiry. Attention to policy making from this perspective is focused on the technical details of systemic efficiency — making things work better without changing the basic structure.

Illustrative is this statement of the problem: "The researcher may easily be tempted into becoming a second-rate pseudophilosopher pontificating on big questions of social needs instead of continuing his painstaking digging into empirical facts by techniques at which he is competent." And "...hard empirical facts of science and economics are the absolute prerequisite to any sensible discussion of policy. A priori ideological argumentation is not policy research, even if the two often tend to be confused with each other." What are "ideological" arguments according to this writer? Social versus private ownership is one such matter that, he observes, "is hard to take...seriously in the 1970s." Another is national sovereignty, a "notion" considered "archaic." (25)

According to this view, efficiency rather than domination should be the center of attention. But the reality of the 1970s imposes another standard. How do women, races, classes, and nations overcome the domination to which they have been, and are, subjected?

Certainly they require facts on which to base their judgments and organize their struggles. But facts in themselves are determined by the ideological framework within which they are

selected as "facts" in the first place. When the political-
philosophical context purposely is left unexamined at the outset,
the facts that are forthcoming can, at best, affect only policy
that leaves unchanged the prevailing structural arrangements.

Communications policy making and the research and planning
that precede it can surely promote a more efficient status quo —
and this is the direction in which most such work has been
pointing. Without fundamental system-questioning, alternate social models cannot be imagined, much less introduced. In the
struggle against domination, the first need, after awareness itself, is the enunciation of alternative social forms. Economic
realities will still have to be taken into account. But they may
be less limiting in the face of different conceptions of what is
necessary, what is desirable, and what is human.

What, then, would constitute a communications/cultural policy
in a national setting that sought to diminish domination, whether
it was imposed internally or externally? Perhaps it is easier
to describe first what such a policy should not be. We may be
uncertain about the features of a nondominating communications
system, but there is much less difficulty in identifying the characteristics and trademarks of domination.

It may be accepted at the outset that the forms, expressions,
and general structure of Western, capitalist communications
cannot be adopted intact as an appropriate model in societies
seeking cultural liberation — though this model is continually
offered by Western analysts and researchers.

It is not easy to ignore the Western communications system
and its products. The system is powerful and possesses the
means to present itself and its products globally. Moreover,
the virtuosity of the instrumentation, combined with expensive,
expertly made material, make the entire operation appear the
essence of modernity, vigor, and attractiveness. By comparison, other forms of communication seem primitive and hope-
lessly outmoded. Those who have familiarity with American
marketing are aware of the great attention that is paid to pack-
aging: the wrapping, the lettering, the color, the print size, the

shape, and the style of the container often take precedence over the content. In the communications system as well, the distinction between content and package (form) cannot be ignored. Attention must be centered on what is in the container and the means by which it got there. If and when this is recognized and understood, the ability to evaluate the Western model of communications will be sharpened immeasurably.

Some claim that an expression of support for cultural integrity is equally a defense of traditionalism and reinforces the most conservative and repressive elements in (mostly) poor societies. According to the most influential group of American communications scholars, the Western mass media are the instruments of modernity and social change; and resisting them signifies an opposition to modernization and an endorsement of orthodoxy, illiteracy, and backwardness. (26) Actually, the situation is reversed. The objective of a cultural policy is not merely to exclude material: it is to assist the process of shaping consciousness. In its very essence it is opposed to established, traditional authority.

Fanon (27), years ago, observed that culture could not be seen as a relic, a museum item, something a worshiper exhumed and placed in a showcase. To Fanon and other revolutionary writers, the development and protection of the people's culture came in the process of struggle. It was not embalmed and revered. It was hammered out in the daily confrontations and battles against dominators, domestic and foreign.

Do the views of Amilcar Cabral (28) support traditionalism? He wrote:

> Without any doubt, underestimation of the cultural values of African peoples, based upon racist feelings and upon the intention of perpetuating foreign exploitation of Africans, has done much harm to Africa. But in the face of the vital need for progress, the following attitudes or behaviors will be no less harmful to Africa: indiscriminate compliments; systematic exaltation of virtues without condemning faults; blind acceptance of the values of

the culture, without considering what presently or potentially regressive elements it contains; confusion between what is the expression of an objective and material historical reality and what appears to be a creation of the mind or the product of a peculiar temperament; absurd linking of artistic creations, whether good or not, with supposed racial characteristics; and finally, the non-scientific or ascientific critical appreciation of the cultural phenomenon. (P. 51)

The test of whether defense of cultural sovereignty offers support to reactionary traditionalism is very simple. Cultural/communications liberation is opposed to repressive authority and domination regardless whether it is exercised from within or outside the country. Defenders of the cultural status quo sometimes challenge external authority, but only in order to maintain their own privileged position. Their resistance ceases when the struggle enters the home territory and their own advantages are challenged. Again Cabral (28) has something to say about this matter. Writing about the early phases of the national liberation movement, he notes:

Several traditional and religious leaders join the struggle at the very beginning or during its development, making an enthusiastic contribution to the cause of liberation. But here again vigilance is indispensable; preserving deep down the cultural prejudices of their class, individuals in this category generally see in the liberation movement the only valid means, using the sacrifice of the masses, to eliminate colonial oppression of their own class and to re-establish in this way their complete political and cultural domination of the people. (P. 47)

Total exclusion of nonindigenous communications material is impossible in the present age of interconnected economies and powerful electronic instrumentation that transmits globally. The few actual examples of autarchy in the 1950s and 1960s were unusual, and probably will not be repeated. China, by virtue of her geographic position and language and the unremitting hostility of the United States, had twenty years of relative insulation from Western information. Cuba, too, though not entirely unmolested by North American message transmission in the period since the Cuban revolution, has enjoyed an unusual amount of cultural space for fifteen years because of the embargo imposed by its powerful neighbor, ninety miles away.

Yet total autarchy as a cultural policy is unrealistic and self-denying. (29) The alternatives to external cultural domination lie elsewhere. This statement should not, however, be regarded as a backhanded endorsement of the communication monopolies' principle of the "free flow of information." Far from it! What it suggests, rather, is an awareness of current technico-material realities, a high level of informed selectivity, and a continuing effort toward popular mobilization of indigenous cultural/informational activity.

It is instructive to read what the Cubans, who have been through a literal blockade, have to say about cultural policy making. A report to a cultural congress in Havana in 1971 stressed self-reliance in national cultural efforts as the basis for "a selective assimilation of the world's culture." The report pointed out:

> The rising technological advance of the mass media and its infinite prospects oblige our revolutionary society to fight against the contamination of the air by imperialist ideology through the creation of ideological antibodies to neutralize its lethal effects. The only alternative reality permits is struggle, not asepsis. Hence the imperative need to engage systematically in a series of public debates, analyses, studies and appraisals that will prepare the masses to face critically every form of expression of bourgeois ideology. (30)

Autarchy, except for a few countries enjoying geographic, linguistic, and natural resource sufficiencies, is not a practical matter. Meanwhile, the pressure of deliberate, as well as un-organized, informational/cultural penetration intensifies. Only the most conscious and comprehensive cultural struggle can be expected to deflect ideological subversion and cultural domina-tion. What this implies is yet another principle of resistance — the reinterpretation of history, from a class perspective, made widely accessible to the people.

We have noted that culture is not an accumulation of museum pieces and that opposition to cultural imperialism is not a de-fense of traditionalism. But it is not correct to deduce from these propositions that history begins only with the modern move-ment against domination. In the present-day communications/cultural struggle against domination, the role of history cannot be minimized. It is history that will recall and refresh vital ex-periences deliberately ignored or distorted in the dominators' presentation of the past. Examples abound of both the suppres-sion of information that could have deepened consciousness and the distortion of information that rendered it harmless — or even useful to a continued condition of domination.

Until recently the struggle and experiences of blacks in North America, over a three-hundred-year period, literally did not exist either in the nation's classrooms or in the mass media. Most of their struggle still remains unrevealed. But one of the few achievements of the black movement of the 1960s has been to force, however limitedly, some information and perspectives about the work and lives of blacks into the communications stream of the nation. Similar experiences characterize the women's movement in the United States.

Naturally, the history referred to here is not the account of-fered by the record-keepers of the dominators, as Sheila Row-botham stresses in her aptly titled work Hidden from History. (31) It is the underside of the continuing process of organization and struggle against domination in all forms. It is discovery, more than reinterpretation, of the past, because what is known and publicized is generally presented from the perspective of priv-ilege.

Language, no less than history, has been the instrument of

domination. This fact does not have to be explained to the victims. Women and blacks, for example, are well aware of the
systematic use of words to present unattractive and/or specific
role imagery. The perpetuation of particular linguistic forms
and expressions coincides with the perpetuation of domination
itself. Why should a society that desires to change its economic
and social system continue to use expressions that served the
old social order very well? (32)

Of course, the use of language is double-edged. Language
changes may also diminish critical thinking and confuse people
about what is happening. Pentagon terminology, for example —
"incursion," "protective preemptive strike," etc. — is simply
a tool of domination. But when new social forces assume control in society, it is to be expected that the expressions and
words of the preceding social order will eventually be eliminated, if for no other reason than that they have diminished ap-
plicability.

The way in which technology is viewed may well constitute
one of the most critical problems for those concerned with creating a liberating communications policy, because the question
of technology interacts with every aspect of contemporary consciousness. As we have noted in the preceding essay, technology, from its origin to its introduction, most often is firmly in
the hands of one or another section of the class that dominates
the social order at the time. And this control directly influences
the character, application, utilization, early modification, and
development of the new equipment or process.

It is not the intention here to insist that new technology must
be avoided, rejected, or minimized in elaborating communications-
cultural policies, whose purpose is to assist the formation
of critical consciousness. Just as cultural autarchy cannot
by itself be productive, indiscriminate rejection of technology
is an admission of helplessness and discouragement. What is
required is the recognition, throughout the decision-making sector, that technology is a social construct. It is not neutral. It
bears the marks of the social order that produced it. The least
people bent on new social relationships can do is to carefully

examine, weigh, and debate the utility of adopting or incorporating, or of modifying, this or that item, process, instrument, or technique taken from an "advanced" society.

Other than in the matter of easily recognizable (no simple qualification), life-saving, and protecting processes and instrumentation — some medical and agricultural practices, for instance — the people's interest may best be served by decisions that are unhurried, deliberate, and critical. Especially to be taken into account are the unique needs — and in each country they are unique — of the people and the recognition that techniques and machinery operative in one set of social relationships, with specific social objectives, may not be appropriate in another.

If the goals and structures of Western capitalism are deemed desirable, it is consistent to import Western techniques and machinery. If another model is sought, however uncertain its ultimate contours may be, it is prudent to exercise extreme caution before embarking on a wholesale reproduction of the modes of production of a market system.

It is indicative of the power of contemporary domination that opposition to its authority is identified as reactionary and unprogressive. If, for example, the "free flow of information" processed and transmitted by a score of cultural corporations of a few Western states is challenged, freedom itself is claimed to be imperiled.

It is helpful, therefore, for those who resist the system of domination to recognize the power that control of the definitional process confers. It is confusing and disorienting, but inevitable, that those struggling toward critical consciousness are continually cast in roles and associated with concepts that are the antithesis of what they are really hoping to achieve. False labeling and the attribution of distorted goals are constant products of the dominators' consciousness-shaping machinery.

Hence the first step in the direction of regaining definitional control — the resistance to domination — is to try not to yield certain crucial, definitional terrain. Words and concepts that have motivated human beings over the centuries toward becoming

more human cannot be relinquished to the ideological dominators without a struggle. "Internationalism," for example, when
used to describe the operations of the multinational corporation,
in the guise of world citizen, should be challenged. At the same
time, efforts to overcome the penetrative power of these monopolistic giants should avoid, as much as possible, being identified
as narrow, nationalistic, and small-gauged strivings.

A communications/cultural policy is national only in its immediate locus of activity, which conforms to the geographic
boundaries of the nation. In its essence, it is profoundly international. It recognizes, respects, and desires to enhance people's liberation efforts to achieve critical consciousness
wherever they are undertaken.

Though there have been many lapses in genuine international
solidarity of peoples in recent decades, the principle is a noble
and enduring one. In the informational field, where the struggle
for liberation is urgent, internationalism is not a marginal issue, a trivial appendage to what is considered central. It is un-
imaginable to seek the liberation of individual consciousness in
a national context that denies or ignores human solidarity
against domination everywhere.

In the actual creation of a comprehensive communications
policy, the definition of news, for example, may constitute one
practical yardstick of the degree to which authentic internationalism motivates the news effort. Understanding of and identifi-
cation with worldwide liberation movements and the struggle
against imperialism in all its forms necessitate the elimination
of present Western television and radio news formats (imitated
practically everywhere). Fragmented, minute, antihistorical
accounts, when reported at all, are the daily filler of what is
supposed to be general broadcasting information.

In the elaboration of an overall communications policy, it is
not necessary to set down a detailed, approved, political guide-
book. If the opposition to domination is genuine, it is perilous
to continue to utilize the techniques of informational control.
What, exactly, will replace radio and television "news" as it
now functions may not be able to be fully answered at this time.

At this point what is important, and needs to be realized, is that the present techniques are useful only in suppressing awareness and for maintaining the governors. Overturning the social pyramid requires new formats, new content, and an over-arching international perspective.

As we have noted earlier, one of the factors in the emergence of the quest for communications policies in many countries has been the increasing numerical and qualitative significance of knowledge workers — professionals, engineers, journalists, broadcasters, editors, and others — in the general labor force. Their numbers, in the industrialized states, continue to multiply.

It may be useful to examine a few of the issues that have developed in this admittedly still nontypical, but increasingly important, segment of the working force. For it is here, at least, that we have a dim perception of what the shape of the future may be as raw economic conditions impose themselves on the consciousness of those working in the consciousness-shaping industries. It seems that two stages can be identified in the evolving struggle in the knowledge industries.

In the first phase — and the experiences of press journalists are being used as the prototype — direct assaults on the workers' economic security occur. Job loss through mergers and the introduction of automatic processes destroy a myth still powerful among nonmanual workers: the notion that the professional worker may advance up the economic ladder to position, status, wealth, and security. (33) Eventually it becomes apparent to some journalists that one of the few ways to achieve minimum work security is to insist on some sort — still not fully formulated — of codetermination. Management's prerogative to make final decisions about the enterprise (newspaper, magazine, publishing company) is questioned.

However, the process does not end here. As the economic crunch intensifies and as the ownership group fights to retain the customary "rights" of capital, stage two emerges. Some knowledge workers begin to see connections between the character and structure of the industry in which they are employed

and their own personal work insecurities and difficulties. When
this occurs, and it happens differentially, one of the strongest
ideological bastions of the system becomes vulnerable. To the
extent that journalists and other information workers recognize
linkages between their specialized jobs and the general matter
of communications control, the myth of objectivity in the market communications system is destroyed. Of course, the process is uneven. It has barely begun to occur in most Western
countries. It is, and will be, fought bitterly on the ideological
front by the ownership class — which will continue to use the
rhetoric of freedom and factuality.

   Another potent weapon of the ownership class in this struggle
is the utilization of the managerial technique of specialization
(professionalism). Capitalist enterprise has used specialization
in production and achieved high levels of productivity. In turn
it has promoted the claim of efficiency as the modus operandi
of the system. Less noticeably, specialization has had an
equally important social and psychological impact. The better-
trained part of the labor force has enjoyed special material
privileges and has basked in the comfort of self-esteem and in-
flated importance.

   In the informational field, as elsewhere, specialization has
been a major factor in producing both a hierarchical structure
in the industry and an elitism and exclusivity in the upper eche-
lons of the profession. These, in turn, nourish most of the ideological biases of capitalism that are embedded in the communications system. What professionalism may mean for those developing countries that accept the concept unquestioningly has
been considered by O'Brien (34): "The process of professionalization in broadcasting may itself have introduced a new constraint resistant to changes in the organizational structure....
There seems no better way of protecting broadcasting training
as it is than arguing against changes which would 'lower the professional standards.'" More fundamentally still, "Changing the
nature of professionalism in the society involves an alteration
of social objectives and rewards which are traditionally in conflict with scientific ones."

If the information system is ever to become a force for liberating consciousness, it cannot remain as it is presently structured — even if editorial workers and journalists and broadcasters were to be given the enlarged participatory rights they
are now beginning to claim. The entire concept of specialization
must be faced and questioned.

The contradiction of extending journalists' participation in
newspaper decision-making, for instance, while at the same
time denying this involvement to the noneditorial staff is a dan-
ger point that current professional workers ignore at their own
long-term peril. The issue is real. It surely will not be missed
by the ownership class when the time it regards as appropriate ar-
rives (as it has in many situations already) to drive wedges between
professionals and nonprofessional workers in the labor force.

The management of the Washington Post, one of the "prestige"
and self-acknowledged liberal newspapers in the United States,
recently provided a model for this tactic. Regrettably, a large
fraction of the editorial and reportial staff allied itself with the
owners against the pressmen, ensuring the defeat of the latter's
strike.

Elitism, specialization, and professionalism are undeniably
utilitarian when the only criterion of performance is profit-
providing efficiency. They are terribly limiting modes of performance when large-scale change is necessary and totally new
means are required to enlist the energies of large numbers of
people previously excluded from any meaningful participation.

Specialization and professionalism serve well to promote the
idea of objectivity, which is the foremost myth of a market communications system. It is not surprising, therefore, that the
structure and the control of the media system are, for the most
part, ignored in journalism and broadcasting schools in the
United States. Professionalism, it need hardly be said, receives
a great deal of attention, and many courses are devoted to its
study.

Though it is hazardous to accept without qualification media
models from the noncapitalist world, the tens of thousands of con-
tributors to the Chinese press — reported by Dallas Smythe (35) —

may be viewed as at least a partial effort to overcome specialization. Similarly, factory papers, wall posters, cinema forums,
and the expanding number of video "freaks" (individualized TV-
production and recording) in the United States are some possibilities of widespread, local participation in the information
process that refute the claim of the necessity for specialization
and professionalism.

All too often even UNESCO is a proponent of the specialization
thesis. Acknowledgment must be made of UNESCO's leading
role in giving prominence to the need for formulating communications policies; but the preference for experts, professionalism, and from-the-top-down policy making evident in UNESCO
papers and documentation on this subject is quite explicit.

The recruiting of specialists, government officials, and academics to plan communications policies may be necessary in the
initial development and promotion of the effort. Restricting participation to these social categories, however, shuts out the popular base from which initiatives have to come if the overall objective — to activate consciousness throughout the society — is
to be realized. At some point a choice has to be made between
professionalism and popular participation.

Specialization, the twin of efficiency, itself depends on differ-
ential training and unequal rewards. It becomes the basis for
hierarchical structuring and elitist concepts, the ultimate
underpinning of domination.

Though it cautions against equating communications policy
with constraint and with "dirigism at the top," UNESCO's Advisory Panel of Consultants on Communications Research rec-
ommends "the setting up of a national communication policy
council" by governments. This council, according to the consultants, "should consist of leaders in the field of politics, specialists in administration, media practitioners and communications research scientists." (36) Where are the working people?
Where are the nonprofessionals? How do initiatives in this proposed council originate? From the top, apparently. No feed-in
from the bottom is recommended.

Again, in another formulation, the experts identified "who is

concerned with communication policies and their formulation."
They listed these categories, in the following order: government executives, legislative bodies, authorities in charge of social and economic planning, individual ministries and their
planning boards, communication enterprises, professional organizations, and, last, the citizen. The experts noted, when they
finally got around to including him/her, that "the citizen has a
direct stake in communication policies." (37)

Paulo Freire (38) observes, "The Right needs an elite who
think for it, assisting it in accomplishing its projects. Revolutionary leadership needs the people in order to make the revolutionary project a reality, but the people in the process of becoming more and more critically conscious." Freire adds that
this process of developing critical consciousness continues to
be indispensable after the revolutionary reality is inaugurated
to dispel the myths that still cling to the people's consciousness, to resist the tendency for the growth of bureaucracy, and
to understand the new technology, which is important for social
development, but which must not be allowed to become en-
shrouded in mystery and removed from popular control.

National communications policy making is a generic term for
the struggle against cultural and social domination in all its
forms, old and new, exercised from within or outside the nation.
It arises with the development of people's critical consciousness and, in the process of struggle, contributes to the development of that consciousness. Consequently, communications-
cultural planning cannot be formulated by experts and delivered
to the rest of the population as a legislative gift.

Specialists and administrators may provide leadership in the
initial stages of the undertaking; but for the effort to begin to
approach a level of widespread development of critical consciousness, the fullest participation of the total community is indispensable. Anything less will make the likelihood of diversion
and atrophy inevitable.

A final word: It is always tempting to believe that an announced goal is a fixed, if distant, point. The attainment of
critical consciousness is not an ultimate destination, but an

ongoing process whose unfolding will continually surprise and confound the patterns of thought and habit that prevail at each point along the historical road of human development. Current efforts at communications-cultural policy making must be seen and understood in this way. However advanced or primitive the formulations may be, they are only markers on an endless road to the realization of human potential.

AFTERWORD

CHILE: COMMUNICATIONS POLICIES
OF REFORM AND COUNTERREVOLUTION

The recent experience of Chile bears out the belief (expressed previously) that in many countries communications-cultural policy making is becoming, or has become, the arena of intensified social struggle. Indeed, in Chile, where a socialistically minded but actually quite reformist government was overthrown and replaced by a harshly repressive regime of authority and property, a critical part of the battle, preceding the actual coup, was waged in and over the mass media. Not without cause was the heavy United States intervention against the Allende Government concentrated in its clandestine support of the opposition press and media. (1)

Freedom of information disappeared in Chile with the coup in September 1973. The ruling junta enforces a rigid code of censorship. In contrast, the media system operating between 1971 and 1973 in the Popular Unity Government period offered an example of pluralism that probably was unique then, if not today.

Under the Popular Unity Government Chileans enjoyed what Western political leadership claims it seeks to promote — an almost unrestricted flow of information representing all shades of the political spectrum. The regime that ousted it represents, again by Western standards, the repudiation of freedom of information.

A perplexing question arises. Why was the relatively pure model of a free marketplace of ideas that the Popular Unity Government tolerated, if not encouraged, so maligned by its opponents within and outside Chile, particularly since one of the strongest political supports of the private enterprise system, in industrial economies, is the appearance of informational diversity and a media system that seems to be open? (2)

As an answer is sought to this question, another puzzle emerges, one we shall take up further along: How warranted, if at all, was the respect the Allende Government bestowed on the objective and practice of maintaining a "free" flow of information, unaccountable to social control?

In the brief period of the Popular Unity Government, no medium was dominated by one political or cultural current. Television, for example, presented the government's position over state and university channels. In terms of audience reached, however (always the major desideratum of media programming in the West), the largest number of viewers watched a commercial channel, carrying material that was largely antisocialist and heavily saturated with commercial programs from the United States ("The FBI," "Mission Impossible," etc.).

Neil P. Hurley (3), no special partisan of the Allende Government, reviewing the media situation that existed at that time, wrote:

What is striking is the increased commercialization of both the state channel 7 and the three university channels, 4, 9 and 13, during the three years of Allende's government...the number of telenovelas — that is Latin TV "soap operas" — increased, and they were clearly impregnated with what Marxists called bourgeois values. Furthermore U.S. imports increased — Julie [sic], Bonanza, Mannix, Paul Lynde, Fred Astaire, Dean Martin and the Doris Day shows. One must see these programs in a socialist atmosphere to realize how ideological they are — the upper and middle class values and personalities, the American living room, kitchen, bathroom and bedroom, and the aura of an escalator standard of living.

Radio was opened up to socialist viewpoints, but most of the stations remained in the hands of propertied and antigovernment influences. The press, too, ranged from left to right; but the number of conservative papers increased during the Allende years.

A socialist perspective appeared for the first time in a sizable range of popular magazines, published with government support. But here as well the wide availability of the commercial periodicals and comic books provided tough competition to the new material, with its unfamiliar and critical orientation. (4)

Despite continual alarms and scares in the international press and inside the country as well, Chile, under Allende, was a country in which every viewpoint found expression. The conservative and propertied organs of opinion, rather than being restricted, carried on an incendiary campaign against the government. Landis (5), a reporter in the country at the time, listed some of the headlines, editorials, and general articles appearing in 1972 in El Mercurio, the main conservative newspaper in the country:

Editorials in El Mercurio

July 26: Innocent child transformed into guerrilla who fights against his parents. Children spy on their parents in socialist countries.

July 28: End of dream of Fidel Castro. Economic chaos in Cuba.

July 31: Editorial critical of Cuba.

August 1: Christian Democrats are hypocrites for accusing us of using scare tactics in election.

August 3: The failure of the Castro regime. Terrorism. The Revolutionary vertigo. The fatal moment (all four editorials about Cuba).

News headlines

July 26: Bolivian guerrillas — trained in Cuba. Chilean guerrillas — in Bolivia. Bolivian guerrilla leaders in Chile.

July 27: Bolivian guerrillas will go to Cuba for Chile.

July 28: Castro — "The future will be worse." Bolivian guerrillas leave for Cuba — from Chile...

It is true, too, that socialist thinking received a greater opportunity for dissemination across the nation than previously.
And this, I believe, offers an explanation for the unrelenting
hostility shown by the anti-Allendists toward the media liberty
prevailing between 1971 and September 1973.

When, as a result of the emergent strength of popular forces,
a genuinely open forum for ideas does develop, in which a systematic exposition of critical thinking can challenge conventional, property views, those espousing the latter find the competition, if it leads to social action, intolerable. It is then that
the status-quo-oriented media protest the condition they always
claim to defend. Thus the actual meaning of the terms "pluralistic" and "free" as they are invoked in private-propertied societies is revealed. When popular awareness has been sharpened and the general apathy ordinarily engendered by formalis-
tic democracy has been dissipated — and the Allende interval
constituted such a time — the enthusiasm of the propertied
classes for a genuinely pluralistic informational environment
vanishes.

Another significant lesson of the Chilean experience for those
concerned with communications policy making is the overwhelming and inseparable interrelatedness of the informational system
with the entire economy. The property-owning class feels secure with informational pluralism when the rest of the cultural
apparatus is firmly in its hands. When the work sites, the
schools, the armed forces, the professional organizations, and
the unions are fulfilling their properly assigned roles of system
reinforcement, fairly wide-ranging informational exchanges in
selected media are acceptable and even useful to the maintenance of stability and legitimacy.

But when the social process and class forces create pressures that interfere with the orderly functioning of a good part
of the social machinery — when, for example, a far-reaching
income redistribution is undertaken, some factories are put under worker control, and a part of the peasantry is organized and
aroused to demand basic reforms on the land — in short, when
the assumptions and the security of the prevailing system of

property and organizational structure are challenged directly across the entire economy — then full debate on the future of the social order becomes intolerable to the privileged classes. And this is understandable. The discussion at this point is no longer just a debate: it is a meaningful process that may very well lead to direct and decisive social and economic change.

Most mass communications in capitalist societies are non-threatening because they are embedded in a network of rein-forcing institutions. These pervasive structures and networks of influence emphasize the media's stabilizing messages. The occasionally dissonant outputs that sometimes (for credibility's sake) emanate from the informational channels are generally ignored. When the reinforcing apparatuses — the functions of the state, the rights of ownership established by law, the orga-nization of learning in the schools — are themselves challenged and brought under critical scrutiny, freewheeling media activity is no longer so acceptable to the customary beneficiaries of propertied democracy. More recently, and for a brief period, developments in Portugal have offered similar instruction.

A related issue that deserves attention and derives also from the Chilean experience is the confusion, still present in many minds, that associates individual freedom and creative talent with the information that now flows through advanced, Western, industrial society. It makes sense that the most influential rep-resentatives of property use the argument of freedom of infor-mation as one of the main supports and attractions of market-style democracy and, obversely, against any alternate form of social organization.

The effort of U.S. multinational corporations to attach global significance to the demand for a free flow of information is an extension of the same principle to the international sphere.

Yet it is now apparent, or it should be, that the free-flow con-cept that was tolerated, and even supported, by the Popular Unity Government in Chile is a spurious principle. It conceals the real power relations between and within nations, and it ob-scures the process by which most cultural and informational messages are now manufactured in the technically developed, capitalist economies.

The flow of information and communications among countries — even, to a certain extent, with respect to the socialistically organized countries — follows the international division of labor, which itself is determined by the structure and practices of the strongest capitalist states. Those economies with the most powerful media-informational combines monopolize and direct the stream of international message transmission. The international traffic in television programs is dominated by a handful of industrialized states, mostly market-organized. The control of the international distribution of films is even more concentrated, and has been in the grip of American capital for more than fifty years. International press and television news flows also are under the control of a few Anglo-American agencies and corporations. So, too, are mass-circulation news and opinion magazines, comic books, book translations, encyclopedias, and even toys and games. These are all part of the international traffic in image and information commodities (6), directed largely by a few commercial corporations in the advanced industrial countries, the United States, in particular.

The free-flow-of-information doctrine undergirds the prevailing pattern of international exchange of information. It legitimates and reinforces the capability of a few dominant economies to impose their cultural definitions and perspectives on the rest of the world, all in the name of noninterference with an allegedly independent and free individual talent.

The conditions of cultural production in the advanced capitalist nations, however, make it ludicrous to accept the view that the cultural messages that are produced in these economies originate and are developed by individual writers, authors, directors, and creative people, all of them independent of the "leisure time" industries that now process most of the cultural imagery moving into national and international "markets."

Listed for the first time in the 1972 Fortune directory of the 500 largest manufacturing corporations, and with a special editorial justification, were some of the major information-cultural corporations in the United States. CBS, ABC, MCA, and Columbia Pictures joined old-time communications conglomerates such as RCA, Westinghouse, and GE in the select group of American super-manufacturing companies.

The description of contemporary Western culture as the artistic product of individuals is appealing but deceitful. Similar obscurantist practice occurs in the economic sphere. There, tiny, retail businesses are regularly equated with massive, multinational corporations; and both are thrown together statistically in an undifferentiated grouping termed "individual business enterprise." The motive for these confusing definitions and misleading aggregations is simple. These vague categories conceal where the locus of power actually is in society. At the same time, their use is an attempt to mobilize on behalf of the supercorporations the popular support that exists for individual and small-scale activity. The claim is always made that the monopolistic aggregations of capital are no different from the individual producers, or writers, or tiny business units that they have either replaced or absorbed.

The cultural conglomerates that preside over information and general message creation cannot be regarded, as they are in the United States, as individuals — persons protected by constitutional guarantees of freedom of speech and expression. RCA, General Electric, CBS, and the Reader's Digest, for example, are not single individuals whose personal rights are inviolable. They are, first and foremost, private, profit-making corporations whose outputs are processed entirely according to commercial specifications. Certainly, individual efforts are incorporated into cultural commodities; but the final product is a corporate package containing corporate ideological concepts.

Consider a recent study by a congressional committee in the United States on Disclosure of Corporate Ownership. (7) It revealed that a few, powerful, New York banks exercised substantial voting rights in American television network and broadcast companies. For example,

Chase Manhattan Bank has sole or partial voting rights to more than 14 per cent of the stock in the Columbia Broadcasting System, as well as 4.5 per cent of the stock in RCA Corporation, parent of the National Broadcasting

Company; Bankers Trust has voting rights to more than
10 per cent of the stock in American Broadcasting Company and 9.8 per cent of the stock in Metromedia; First
National City Bank (of New York) has voting rights to 7.1
per cent of the stock in Capital Cities Broadcasting Corporation, which includes six TV and eleven radio stations;
eleven banks have voting rights to 34.1 per cent of the
common stock in ABC...

Can image-making and image-disseminating enterprises, under banking and industrial capital domination, justifiably be regarded as individuals with inalienable rights? In fact, the products of the cultural industry are far more deserving of the most
searching public scrutiny than are the ordinary commodities
produced for the general consumer market. It is true that many
consumer goods emphasize and frequently embody the acquisi-
tive and individualistic character of the society producing them
(the gas-eating, rubber-consuming automobile, for instance).
As such they are rarely, if ever, value free. But the outputs of
the consciousness-shaping industries are, in their essence, ideological. Woe to the community whose social policy fails to recognize this central point.

   To believe that the product manufactured by the American
film industry, for example, is only for diversion and basically
without social meaning is to ignore, willfully, one of the most
powerful forms of cultural domination. Indeed, the Chilean dic-
tatorship has not been confused about this. One of its first "cultural" initiatives after the coup was to reopen Chilean markets
to U.S. films and thus, in the words of junta General Leigh,
"end the nightmare of Marxist cinema." (8) (Actually, American films were by no means absent from Chilean screens
throughout the Allende period. In 1971, Love Story, Tora, Tora,
Tora, Walt Disney productions, and John Wayne films, among
others, were exhibited prominently in Santiago theaters.)

   This is not to suggest that all cultural products in an advanced capitalist society are single-mindedly fashioned to impose an ideology favorable to the system's dominators. Often

this is true — particularly in some media lines. It is also understandable that the cultural industries must take into account the social realities of the time. To do this effectively it is necessary that material be presented that at least touches on some of the potentially explosive issues of the day. This means, according to Stuart Hall (9), incorporating the contradictions of the social setting into the message itself.

But under no circumstances are the contradictions made explicit or presented in a manner that really clarifies the social condition. That some individuals will recognize a critical problem, even in its most obscure presentation, is a windfall — but it is no reason to believe that the media are acting as their own (and the system's) grave-diggers.

As might be expected, the proponents of a free flow of information, consistent with their position of recognizing no limits to the circulation of corporate-cultural outputs, are also strong critics of national sovereignty. To the directors of the multinational corporations, national sovereignty is a painful and disagreeable condition that they would do their utmost to reduce, or at least dominate. Yet in the communications-cultural sphere, national sovereignty is the last defense against the forward march of the media conglomerates. If the barrier of sovereignty goes down, there is absolutely no protection left to hold back a sweeping take-over of the physical hardware, the communications structures, and the entire media content by a clutch of world-girdling, private, cultural monopolies.

Chile under Allende made a few moves in the direction of defending its cultural integrity. A wider spread of film importations was encouraged, and the almost exclusive reliance on U.S. movies was reduced. The activities of the advertising agencies, especially those employed by the powerful, multinational companies, were curtailed or drastically limited. State book and periodical publishing houses were created, and national and progressive themes were introduced into popular and mass-circulation publications. (10) Yet, in retrospect, these were small steps and pathetically limited. (11) In fact, during the same period, Reader's Digest, in its Chilean edition, continued to sell 100,000 copies a month.

What, then, may we conclude from the Chilean experience with respect to the overall informational-communications sector? Future national efforts at social transformation will recognize the necessity for bold and rapid decision-making in the communications-cultural spectrum in two directions simultaneously.

One thrust will be directed against the external, dominating network of media information. Included here will be advertising, public relations, market research, polling, and the entire range of imported media products, from films, to books, to TV programs. The emphasis, if it is rational, will rest entirely on the materials and structures of domination.

Xenophobia, perhaps not easy to avoid in practice, is inconsistent with true cultural integrity. The issue is not foreign cultural imagery, but messages of domination, whatever their origin. The Reader's Digest, for example, would hardly pass muster in a serious social transformation, not because it is produced largely in the United States, but because it is saturated with the ideology of individual selfishness, pro-monopoly business, hostility to the basic needs of working people, and jingoistic militarism — to list but a few of its constant themes.

A second front in the cultural-communications transformation will no doubt move rapidly to the creation of alternate media structures and products in ways that promote widespread popular participation.

To combine both these efforts is a very large order indeed — especially when there are, to date, no totally satisfactory models to emulate. The closest examples may be the guerrilla and liberation army techniques of community involvement. (12)

As these examples relate to particular situations or to nations at differing levels of development, it is by no means assured that the specific techniques utilized in one country are appropriate or even transferable to another. What is essential is the recognition of the nature and the design of the efforts, so that with modification they may be adapted to the changed circumstances of place and the historical point of development.

Clearly, widespread popular participation is an indispensable and fundamental component of the process of alternative mass communication. Whatever means or method encourages as many individuals as possible to participate and take a personal interest in the informational process is potentially worthy of application. In this regard, borrowing from the all too familiar genres, styles, and formats of the now dominant, hierarchical communications-culture imposes a perilous burden on a newly emerging social system.

The arguments of pluralism, too, as we have seen, must be viewed warily. What is most frequently presented as pluralism is, in most instances, merely another facet of the basic cultural industry, organized commercially and anchored ideologically to private ownership and a way of life most conducive to its maintenance.

In sum, the cultural-communication-policy conclusions that derive from the Chilean experience are mainly these:

1. Pluralism in communication conceals class domination. When that domination is seriously threatened, pluralism is rejected by those who usually extol its virtues.

2. The messages of the dominating system are corporately organized and commercially disseminated. Their claim to circulate on the basis of individual freedom of expression is invalid.

3. The obligation to defend the nation's informational-cultural sovereignty is not a call to narrow provincialism and compartmentalization. It is an assertion of resistance to the penetrative power of the multinational corporations. Consequently, national and socialist cultural policies are an essential prerequisite of cultural integrity.

4. Heightened individual consciousness is both an essential element in and the outgrowth of the liberating/revolutionary process. It is not an automatic benefit of improved or sophisticated new communications technology. On the contrary, special attention and extra effort are required to ensure the possibility of using advanced technology for social ends. The liberating process must recognize, at all times, the importance of the

communications/information component and try to develop appropriate means of fostering individual participation and engagement in the communication effort. This is not a one-time effort. Too many sad historical examples reveal either a once-developed or a partially developed popular consciousness that has become atrophied. With its disappearance has come a reversion to manipulative informational control. Participation may be the only means of developing and maintaining individual and group consciousness and thus keeping alive the dynamic of change and renewal.

NOTES

1. <u>Cultural Domination: Sources, Context,</u>
<u>and Current Styles</u>

1) Immanuel Wallerstein, "Class-Formation in the Capitalist World-Economy," paper presented at the VIIIth World Congress of Sociology, Toronto, August 18-24, 1974, pp. 1-2.

2) David Ogilvy, "Confessions of a Magazine Reader," <u>Reader's Digest</u> promotional brochure, September 1974.

3) Herbert I. Schiller, <u>Mass Communications and American Empire</u>, New York, Kelley, 1969; and <u>The Mind Managers</u>, Boston, Beacon Press, 1973.

4) William H. Read, <u>Transnational Mass Media</u>. To be published.

5) Karl P. Sauvant, "The Potential of Multinational Enterprises as Vehicles for the Transmission of Business Culture," in Karl P. Sauvant and F. G. Lavit (Eds.), <u>The Politics of Multinational Enterprises</u>, Frankfurt, Herder and Herder. In press.

6) Elizabeth Fox de Cardona and Luis Ramiro Beltran, "Towards the Development of a Methodology to Diagnosis [sic] Public Communications Institutions," paper presented at the International Broadcast Institute General Meeting, Cologne, September 1-4, 1975, p. 29.

7) David Kunzle, "Introduction to the English Edition," in Ariel Dorman and Armand Mattelart, <u>How to Read Donald Duck: Imperialist Ideology in the Disney Comic</u>, New York,

110

International General, 1975, p. 14.

8) Raymond B. Nixon, Education for Journalism in Latin America, New York, Council on Higher Education in the American Republics, Institute of International Education, 1971.

9) Leroy Pope, "Business Schools Go Multinational," San Diego Evening Tribune, August 15, 1975, Section A-15.

10) Karl P. Sauvant, op. cit.

11) Rita Cruise O'Brien, "Domination and Dependence in Mass Communication: Implications for the Use of Broadcasting in Developing Countries," IDS Discussion Paper No. 64, Brighton, England, University of Sussex, Institute of Development Studies, October 1974.

12) Juan E. Corradi, "Cultural Dependence and the Sociology of Knowledge: The Latin American Case," International Journal of Contemporary Sociology, 1971, 8(1), 35-55.

13) Louis A. Perez, Jr., "Tourism in the West Indies," Journal of Communication, 1975, 25(2), 136-43.

14) Time, June 30, 1975, pp. 55-56.

15) Dave Anderson, "Malaysian Promoter Has a Way with Money," International Herald Tribune, June 27, 1975.

16) Evelina Dagnino, "Cultural and Ideological Dependence: Building a Theoretical Framework," in F. Bonilla and Robert Girling (Eds.), Struggles of Dependency, Stanford, Calif., 1973.

17) Tilford Gaines, Economic Report, New York, Manufacturers Hanover Trust, October 1975.

18) Hamid Mowlana, "Trends in Research on International Communication in the United States," Gazette (Amsterdam), 1973, 19(2), 79-90.

19) Glen H. Fisher, Public Diplomacy and the Behavioral Sciences, Bloomington, Ind., Indiana University Press, 1972.

20) Wilson P. Dizard, "Which Way to the Future?," USIA Communicator, 1973, 1(4) (July), 11-13.

21) Robert A. Rosenblatt, "Northrup Gets $60 Million Hike on Iran Job: Profit Still in Doubt," Los Angeles Times, September 6, 1973.

22) See, for instance, the publications of the Aspen Institute Program on Communications and Society, especially the con-

tributions of Leonard Marks and Ithiel de Sola Pool in Control of the Direct Broadcast Satellite: Values in Conflict, Palo Alto, Calif., Aspen Institute, Program on Communications and Society, in association with the Office of External Research, U.S. Department of State, 1974.

23) International Information, Education, and Cultural Relations: Recommendations for the Future, Washington, D.C., Georgetown University, Center for Strategic and International Studies, 1975, p. 12.

2. The Diplomacy of Cultural Domination
   and the Free Flow of Information

1) John S. Knight, "World Freedom of Information," speech presented in Philadelphia, Pa., April 16, 1946. Published in Vital Speeches, 1946, 12, 472-77.

2) Palmer Hoyt, "Last Chance," speech delivered before the Jackson County Chamber of Commerce, Medford, Oregon, September 18, 1945. Published in Vital Speeches, 1946, 12, 60-62.

3) James Lawrence Fly, "A Free Flow of News Must Link the Nations," Free World, 1944, 8(2) (August), 165-69.

4) Business Week, 1945, 87 (August 4), 32, 34, 41.

5) Quoted in "Charter for a Free Press," Newsweek, December 11, 1944, p. 88.

6) Department of State Bulletin, 1946, 14(344) (February 3), 160.

7) Quoted by John S. Knight, op. cit., p. 476.

8) Report of the United States Delegates to the United Nations Conference on Freedom of Information, U.S. Department of State Publication 3150, International Organization and Conference Series 111.5, Washington, D.C., U.S. Government Printing Office, 1948.

9) John S. Knight, op. cit., pp. 472-73.

10) Kirk H. Porter and Donald Bruce Johnson, National Party Platforms, 1840-1964, Urbana, Ill., and London, Univer-

sity of Illinois Press, 1966, pp. 404, 413.

11) Congressional Record, 90th Congress, 8044:58 Stat.
(Pt. 2), 1119.

12) The New York Times, November 29, 1944.

13) Editor and Publisher, December 2, 1944, p. 7.

14) The New York Times, November 29, 1944.

15) Editor and Publisher, June 16, 1945, pp. 5, 64.

16) Editor and Publisher, April 21, 1945, p. 15.

17) Report of the United States Delegation to the Inter-
American Conference on Problems of War and Peace (Mexico
City, Mexico, February 21-March 8, 1945), U.S. Department of
State Publication 2497, Conference Series 85, Washington, D.C.,
U.S. Government Printing Office, 1946, p. 21.

18) Proposed Educational and Cultural Organization of the
United Nations, U.S. Department of State Publication 2382,
Washington, D.C., U.S. Government Printing Office, 1945,
pp. 5-7.

19) Luther H. Evans, The United States and UNESCO; A Sum-
mary of the United States Delegation Meetings to the Constitutional Conference of the United Nations Educational, Scientific
and Cultural Organization, in Washington and London, October-
November 1945, Dobbs Ferry, N.Y., Oceana Publications,
1971, p. 11.

20) Report of the United States Commission for the United
Nations Educational, Scientific and Cultural Organization to the
Secretary of State, 1947.

21) See Llewellyn White and Robert D. Leigh, Peoples Speak-
ing to Peoples. A Report on International Mass Communications
from the Commission on Freedom of the Press, Chicago, University of Chicago Press, 1946.

22) First Session of the General Conference of the United Na-
tions Educational, Scientific and Cultural Organization, Paris,
November 19-December 10, 1946. Report of the United States
Delegation, with Selected Documents, Washington, D.C., U.S.
Government Printing Office, 1947, p. 17.

23) Resolution 2/9 of 21 June 1946, Economic and Social
Council, Official Records (First Year, Second Session), Lake

Success, N.Y., United Nations, No. 8, p. 400.

24) Yearbook on Human Rights for 1947, Lake Success, N.Y., United Nations, 1949, p. 439.

25) William Benton (chairman, United States delegation to the Freedom of Information Conference), address delivered before the Anglo-American Press Club, Paris, France, April 7, 1948. Published in Department of State Bulletin, April 18, 1948, pp. 518-20.

26) "Accomplishments of the United Nations Conference on Freedom of Information," Documents and State Papers (U.S. Department of State), 1948, 1(3) (June).

27) United Nations documents E/Conf. 6/79 and E/1050, August 28, 1948.

28) John B. Whitton, "The United Nations Conference on Freedom of Information and the Movement Against International Propaganda," American Journal of International Law, 1949, 43 (January), 76.

29) Economist, May 1, 1948, p. 701.

30) Thomas Guback, The International Film Industry, Bloomington, Ind., Indiana University Press, 1969.

31) Kaarle Nordenstreng and Tapio Varis, Television Traffic — A One-Way Street?, Reports and Papers on Mass Communication, No. 70, Paris, UNESCO, 1974.

32) Herbert I. Schiller, The Mind Managers, Boston, Beacon Press, 1973.

33) Intermedia, 1973, No. 3, p. 1 (a publication of the International Broadcast Institute).

34) Robert D. Leigh, "Freedom of Communication Across National Boundaries," Educational Record, 1948, 29 (October), 381-91.

35) Report of the Working Group on Direct Broadcast Satellites of the Work of Its Fourth Session, A/AC. 105/117, New York, United Nations, 22 June 1973, Annex 1, p. 1.

36) UNESCO Declaration of Guiding Principles on the Use of Satellite Broadcasting for the Free Flow of Information, Spread of Education and Greater Cultural Exchange, document A/AC. 105/109, 1972 (mimeographed).

37) Frank Stanton, "Will They Stop Our Satellites?", The New York Times, October 22, 1972, Section 2 (Arts & Leisure), pp. 23, 39.

38) Earl L. Vance, "Freedom of the Press for Whom?", Virginia Quarterly Review, 1945, 21 (Summer), 340-54.

39) John Scali, U.S. delegate to the UN, in a speech before the General Assembly, as reported in The New York Times, December 7, 1974.

40) The New York Times, Editorial, November 23, 1974.

41) The New York Times, December 12, 1974.

42) Final Recommendations of the Helsinki Consultations, Helsinki, Government of Finland, 1973, p. 15.

43) Conference on Security and Cooperation in Europe, Verbatim Records, Part 1, CSCE/I/PV.5, Helsinki, 5 July 1973, Sir Alec Douglas-Home.

44) Urho Kekkonen, "The Free Flow of Information: Towards a Reconsideration of National and International Communication Policies," address before Symposium on the International Flow of Television Programmes, University of Tampere, Tampere, Finland, May 21, 1973.

3. The Technology of Cultural Domination

1) Kaarle Nordenstreng and Herbert I. Schiller, "Helsinki: The New Equation," Journal of Communication, 1976, 26(1), 130-34.

2) Analysis of Problems and Table of Objectives To Be Used as a Basis for Medium-Term Planning (1977-1982), document 18C/4, Paris, UNESCO, 1974, p. 28.

3) Leonard H. Marks, "International Conflict and the Free Flow of Information," in Control of the Direct Broadcast Satellite: Values in Conflict, Palo Alto, Calif., Aspen Institute, Program on Communication and Society, in association with the Office of External Research, U.S. Department of State, 1974, pp. 65-71.

4) Frederick W. Frey, "Communications and Development,"

in Ithiel de Sola Pool et al. (Eds.), Handbook of Communication, Chicago, Rand McNally, 1973, p. 400.

5) Statistics on Radio and Television, 1950-1960 and Statistical Yearbook, 1962, Paris, UNESCO.

6) See Iskandar Alisjahbana, "Technology and Development," paper presented at International Broadcast Institute General Meeting, Mexico City, September 1-5, 1974.

7) Nicholas Garnham, "Trojan Horses: Some Socio-political Implications of Communication Technology," paper presented at International Broadcast Institute General Meeting, Mexico City, September 1-5, 1974.

8) Raymond Williams, Television: Technology and Cultural Form, London, Fontana/Collins, 1974, pp. 13, 19.

9) Dallas Smythe, After Bicycles What?, 1973 (mimeographed).

10) N. Garnham, op. cit.

11) Barry Commoner, The Closing Circle, New York, Bantam, 1972, pp. 266-67.

12) Stanton A. Glantz and Norm V. Albers, "Department of Defense R&D in the University," Science, 1974, 186(4165), 706-11.

13) Herbert I. Schiller, Mass Communications and American Empire, New York, Kelley, 1969.

14) Joseph N. Pelton, INTELSAT: Politics and Functionalism, Mt. Airy, Md., Lomond Books, 1974. See especially pp. 106 and 122.

15) N. Garnham, op. cit.

16) For a thoughtful discussion of this problem, see David Dickson, Alternative Technology, Glasgow, Fontana/Collins, 1974.

17) John Lent, "Mass Media in the Developing World. Four Conundrums," paper presented before the International Association for Mass Communication Research, Leipzig, September 12-20, 1974, p. 4.

18) Nicholas Wade, "Green Revolution. II. Problems of Adapting a Western Technology," Science, 1974, 186(4170), 1186-92.

19) International Herald Tribune, March 23-24, 1974.

20) Tabitha M. Powledge, "Dangerous Research and Public Obligation," The New York Times, August 24, 1974.

21) Leon R. Kass, "The New Biology: What Price Relieving Man's Estate?", Science, 1971, 174(4011), 779-88.

22) Hamid Mowlana, "The Multinational Corporation and the Diffusion of Technology," in A. A. Said (Ed.), The New Sovereigns: Multinational Corporations as World Powers, Englewood Cliffs, N.J., Prentice-Hall, 1975, p. 83.

23) Kathleen Teltsch, "Space Plans Frustrate the Have-Nots," The New York Times, May 14, 1972, p. 13.

24) Gunnar Adler-Karlsson, "The Political Economy of East-West-South Cooperation," unpublished manuscript from the Wiener Institut für Internationale Wirtschaftsvergleichs, 1974, p. 57.

Self-reliance is a policy instrument available to dominators, too, and with less difficulty. The North American reaction to the oil embargo imposed in the fall of 1973 by the oil-producing nations illustrates this very well: "There are times in international life, no less than in personal affairs, when it becomes possible to live satisfactorily with people only when one has demonstrated the capacity to live without them, and this would seem to be one of those times," stated George F. Kennan (quoted by A. N. Spaniel, founder of the International Playtex Corporation, in The New York Times, December 4, 1973).

25) Frantz Fanon, The Wretched of the Earth, New York, Grove Press, 1965, pp. 253-55.

26) D. Smythe, op. cit.

27) I. Alisjahbana, op. cit., p. 10.

28) Juan E. Corradi, "Cultural Dependence and the Sociology of Knowledge: The Latin American Case," International Journal of Contemporary Sociology, 1971, 8(1), 35-55.

29) Votes in the United Nations and UNESCO in 1973 and 1974 on these matters invariably found the United States in almost complete isolation. A report sympathetic to the U.S. position noted: "In its initial insistence that there be no international agreement, the United States stood alone and was even viewed in some quarters with hostility. It had no support from any

other nation, not even those that place a high value on the free flow of information and ideas" (p. 11). Paul L. Laskin and Abram Chayes, "A Brief History of the Issues," in Control of the Direct Broadcast Satellite: Values in Conflict, op. cit., pp. 3-14.

30) Edwin B. Parker, "Technology Assessment or Institutional Changes ?", in G. Gerbner, L. Gross, and W. Melody (Eds.), Communications Technology and Social Policy, New York, Wiley, 1973, p. 541.

31) Ruth M. Davis, editorial in Science, 1975, 188(4185), 213.

4. National Communications Policies:
A New Arena for Social Struggle

1) E. Parker, "Social Implications of Computer/Tele-communications Systems," draft of paper prepared for Session A of the Conference on Computer/Telecommunications, Committee for Scientific and Technological Policy, Organization for Economic Cooperation and Development, Paris, February 4-6, 1975.

2) Government of Finland, Office of the Council of State, June 1972.

3) Proposals for a Communications Policy for Canada, Ottawa, Ontario, Canada, March 1973; The New York Times, January 25, 1975.

4) Report of the Meeting of Experts on Communications Policies and Planning, July 1972, document COM/MD/24, Paris, UNESCO, December 1972.

5) Communications Policies in Hungary, Ireland, Sweden, Yugoslavia, Federal Republic of Germany, Paris, UNESCO, 1974.

6) International Broadcast Institute, Considerations for a European Communications Policy, London, International Broadcast Institute, 1973.

7) Robert Wangermee, "Television, New Broadcasting Techniques and Cultural Development," Memorandum, document

CCC/FES(72) 98, Strasbourg, Council of Europe, October 9, 1972.

8) The Labour Party, The People and the Media, London, 1974.

9) Programme commun de Gouvernement du Parti communiste français et du Parti socialiste (27 Juin 1972), Paris, Editions Sociales, 1972.

10) Communications Policy Workshop, ICODES (Instituto Colombia de Desarrollo Social), Bogota, Colombia, February 23-28, 1975 (mimeographed).

11) Revolution Africaine, 1973, No. 499, 14-20 September.

12) Proposals for a Communications Policy for Canada, op. cit.

13) T. Guback, "Cultural Identity and Film in the European Economic Community," paper presented at conference "Film in Europe," London, February 21-23, 1974.

14) K. Nordenstreng and T. Varis, Television Traffic — A One-Way Street?, Reports and Papers on Mass Communication, No. 70, Paris, UNESCO, 1974.

15) International Economic Report of the President, Transmitted to Congress, February 7, 1974, Washington, D.C., U.S. Government Printing Office, p. 70.

16) Ithiel de Sola Pool, "The Rise of Communications Policy Research," Journal of Communication, 1974, 24(2), 31-42.

17) Raymond Williams, Television: Technology and Cultural Form, London, Fontana/Collins, 1974, p. 19.

18) Social Indicators 1973, Executive Office of the President, Office of Management and Budget, Washington, D.C., U.S. Government Printing Office, 1973, p. 225.

19) F. Kempers, "Democratization and Participation in the Dutch Press," paper presented before the International Association for Mass Communication Research, Leipzig, September 12-20, 1974.

20) Craig R. Whitney, "Bonn Completing a 'Fair' Press Bill," The New York Times, August 18, 1974.

21) Meeting of International Advisory Panel on Communication Research, Paris, UNESCO, October 15-19, 1973. Commu-

nication Research Policies and Planning (résumé of key issues in documents COM/MD/20 and COM/MD/24) (mimeographed working paper), Paris, UNESCO, October 1973, p. 3.

22) Report of the Meeting of Experts on Communications Policies and Planning, op. cit.

23) See the discussion on public opinion polls in Herbert I. Schiller, The Mind Managers, Boston, Beacon Press, 1973.

24) K. Nordenstreng, "Comprehensive Communications Policies — An Example from Finland," Tampere, Finland, 1974 (mimeographed).

25) I. de Sola Pool, op. cit.

26) I. de Sola Pool, "Direct Broadcast Satellites and the Integrity of National Culture," in Control of the Direct Broadcast Satellite: Values in Conflict, Palo Alto, Calif., Aspen Institute, Program on Communications and Society, in association with the Office of External Research, U.S. Department of State, 1974. See also D. Lerner, F. Frey, and W. Schramm, in Handbook of Communication, Chicago, Rand McNally, 1973.

27) Frantz Fanon, The Wretched of the Earth, New York, Grove Press, 1965.

28) A. Cabral, Return to the Source: Selected Speeches of Amilcar Cabral, edited by Africa Information Service, New York, Monthly Review Press, 1973.

29) Still, a forthcoming book by Richard Gott, Guardian correspondent, bears the tentative title Close Your Borders.

30) Speech of the Cuban Minister of Education, Granma, Havana, May 2, 1971.

31) Sheila Rowbotham, Hidden from History, New York, Random House, 1974.

32) A small step toward changing the language of sex domination is observable in the "Guidelines for Equal Treatment of the Sexes in McGraw-Hill Book Company Publications," New York, McGraw-Hill, 1974.

33) For the problems of organizing publishing-industry workers in unions, see T. Powers, "Pride and Prejudice," MORE, 1975, 5(1).

34) Rita Cruise O'Brien, "Domination and Dependence in

Mass Communication: Implications for the Use of Broadcasting in Developing Countries," IDS Discussion Paper No. 64, Brighton, England, University of Sussex, Institute of Development Studies, October 1974, pp. 8-9.

35) Dallas Smythe, "Mass Communications and Cultural Revolution: The Experience of China," in G. Gerbner, L. Gross, and W. Melody (Eds.), Communications Technology and Social Policy, New York, Wiley, 1973.

36) Meeting of International Advisory Panel on Communication Research, December 15-19, 1973, Paris, UNESCO (mimeographed).

37) Report of the Meeting of Experts on Communications Policies and Planning, op. cit.

38) P. Freire, Cultural Action for Freedom, Harmondsworth, Middlesex, England, Penguin, 1972, p. 78.

Afterword

1) "...the CIA covertly channeled $11.5 million to El Mercurio, the largest daily paper in Chile, to insure anti-Allende coverage, to keep the paper solvent. El Mercurio was published...by Augustine Edwards, a close friend of Donald M. Kendall, president of Pepsi Cola" [and an intimate of former President Nixon]. The New York Times, December 5, 1975.

2) John C. and Michele R. Pollock, The U.S. Press and Chile: Ideology and International Conflict, October 1972 (mimeographed).

3) Neil P. Hurley, "Chilean Television: A Case Study of Political Communication," Journalism Quarterly, 1974, 51(4), 683-89, 725.

4) For a discussion of this point, see H. Schiller and D. Smythe, "Chile: An End to Cultural Colonialism," Society, 1972, 9(5), 35-39, 61.

5) Fred Landis, "How the CIA Gets Good Press in Chile," Spectrum (University of Illinois), October 26, 1974. El Mercurio, it will be recalled (see note 1 to this section) was the

CIA's main conduit to the Chilean middle class and served to "destabilize" the Allende Government and prepare the way for the military coup.

6) See Tapio Varis, "International Inventory of Television Programme Structure and the Flow of TV Programmes Between Nations," University of Tampere, Finland, 1973; Thomas Guback, "Film as International Business," Journal of Communication, 1974, 24(1), 90-101; Oliver Boyd-Barrett, "The World-Wide News Agencies," paper presented before the International Association for Mass Communication Research, Leipzig, September 12-20, 1974.

7) Disclosure of Corporate Ownership, prepared by the Inter-Governmental Relations and Budgeting Management and Expenditures group of the Committee on Government Operations, U.S. Senate, December 27, 1973, Washington, D.C., U.S. Government Printing Office, 1973, p. 8.

8) International Herald Tribune, October 4, 1973.

9) Stuart Hall, "External Influences on Broadcasting: The External-Internal Dialectic in Broadcasting: Television's Double Bind," in F. S. Badley (Ed.), Fourth Symposium on Broadcasting Policy, Manchester, University of Manchester, Department of Extramural Studies, 1972.

10) H. Schiller and D. Smythe, op. cit.

11) Patricia Fagen, "The Media in Allende's Chile," Journal of Communication, 1974, 24(1), 59-70.

12) Tran Van Dinh, "Communications and Wars of National Liberation," Journal of Communication, 1976. In press.

INDEX

ABOUT THE AUTHOR

Herbert I. Schiller, educated at the College of the City of New York, Columbia University, and New York University, has been Professor of Communications, Third College, University of California, San Diego, since 1970. He was previously research professor and editor of The Quarterly Review of Economics and Business at the University of Illinois. The holder of a number of fellowships and the author of a wide variety of articles, he has written Mass Communications and American Empire and The Mind Managers, and has edited Superstate: Readings in the Military Industrial Complex.